Make a Great Speech

This book is dedicated to my late father Mr Thomas Peter Forsyth for his courage and bravery when faced with adversity.

Teach® Yourself

Make a Great Speech

Jackie Arnold

For UK order enquiries: please contact Bookpoint Ltd,
130 Milton Park, Abingdon, Oxon OX14 4SB.
Telephone: +44 (0) 1235 827720. Fax: +44 (0) 1235 400454.
Lines are open 09.00–17.00, Monday to Saturday, with a 24-hour
message answering service. Details about our titles and how to
order are available at www.teachyourself.com

For USA order enquiries: please contact McGraw-Hill Customer
Services, PO Box 545, Blacklick, OH 43004-0545, USA.
Telephone: 1-800-722-4726. Fax: 1-614-755-5645.

For Canada order enquiries: please contact McGraw-Hill Ryerson
Ltd, 300 Water St, Whitby, Ontario L1N 9B6, Canada.
Telephone: 905 430 5000. Fax: 905 430 5020.

Long renowned as the authoritative source for self-guided
learning – with more than 50 million copies sold worldwide –
the **Teach Yourself** series includes over 500 titles in the fields of
languages, crafts, hobbies, business, computing and education.

British Library Cataloguing in Publication Data: a catalogue record
for this title is available from the British Library.

Library of Congress Catalog Card Number: on file.

First published in UK 2008 by Hodder Education, part of
Hachette UK, 338 Euston Road, London NW1 3BH.

First published in US 2008 by The McGraw-Hill Companies, Inc.

This edition published 2010.

Previously published as *Teach Yourself Speaking on
Special Occasions*

The **Teach Yourself** name is a registered trade mark of
Hodder Headline.

Copyright © 2008, 2010 Jackie Arnold

Typeset by MPS Limited, a Macmillan Company.

Printed in Great Britain for Hodder Education, an Hachette UK
Company, 338 Euston Road, London NW1 3BH, by CPI Cox &
Wyman, Reading, Berkshire RG1 8EX.

The publisher has used its best endeavours to ensure that the URLs
for external websites referred to in this book are correct and active
at the time of going to press. However, the publisher and the
author have no responsibility for the websites and can make no
guarantee that a site will remain live or that the content will remain
relevant, decent or appropriate.

Hachette UK's policy is to use papers that are natural, renewable
and recyclable products and made from wood grown in sustainable
forests. The logging and manufacturing processes are expected to
conform to the environmental regulations of the country of origin.

Impression number   10 9 8 7 6 5 4 3 2
Year   2014 2013 2012 2011

Contents

Part six: And finally...

Acknowledgements

Thanks go to:

My husband Steve for putting up with late dinners, deep sighs and, on occasion, somewhat distracted behaviour.

My agent Fiona Spenser Thomas for her continued support and encouragement.

The help and support of the Toastmasters International Speakers' Club members who kindly contributed speeches.

David Robertson
Steve Roberts
Marion Way
Adam Broomfield-Strawn
Michelle McManus
John Postlethwaite.

Meet the author

I am a former BBC radio presenter and broadcaster and the founder of Brighton & Hove Speakers' Club, part of Toastmasters International. I am an experienced speaker and give keynote speeches at conferences and events both in the UK and Europe.

I coach a variety of people who want to banish their butterflies and generally improve their public speaking skills. I support people to deliver and write powerful and well-structured speeches.

Speaking can be great fun, seriously stimulating and is an amazing way to improve confidence. This is why I decided to write a book, so you too can 'make a great speech' whatever the occasion.

Whether you are preparing your wedding speech, speaking at your local club, going for an interview, or preparing for a series of work presentations, you will find everything you need right here. Tips and techniques to plan, prepare and practise, advice on how to structure your speech and hints on vocal techniques so you are heard clearly even by those sitting right at the back of the room.

Jackie Arnold

Only got a minute?

Whether you are speaking to a family group, a local club, a large conference, an interview panel or at business events, the skills and techniques are basically the same.

Let's look at a few ideas to start you off:

▸ Determine your objectives.

▸ Ask yourself if you are going to inform, motivate or entertain people. Decide on the length of the speech and what your key topic areas will be.

▸ Ask yourself what you want people to go away with. New information, motivation to take some action, or just a good feeling having had a fun time?

▸ Write down some ideas and start to organize them in a way that suits you best. Select a few relevant points and think about which would be best to start, which would best create the main body of the speech and which to end with.

▸ Starting with a good quote or a brief anecdote can often get people's attention. Ensure it is relevant and underlines your key message. You could end with a surprising fact or short story.

- Maintaining human interest can really enhance your message, even for dry material such as a business review. Mention the names of key people, and weave in a brief story to keep people engaged.

- If appropriate to your topic, bringing in photographs, pictures and props can really add sparkle to any speech. Make sure they are held so that everyone can see them at the back. Remember that everything needs to be bigger on a stage. This includes gestures, voice tone and projection, props and notices.

- To aid your nerves, place a glass of water where you can easily reach it and take a sip if you lose your way. This gives you time to think and regroup. Also, before you speak take time to breathe deeply in and out. This will calm you and send vital oxygen to your brain!

5 Only got five minutes?

Anyone can make a speech. You are more than likely already making mini-speeches every day in some form or another:

▶ facing an interview panel
▶ making a complaint
▶ speaking on the telephone
▶ making an appointment
▶ setting up a bank account
▶ hiring a car.

So, how do you start planning for a longer speech to be made in front of an audience? First, do some research into your topic:

▶ If you are speaking to a family gathering you may need to approach some of the relations to get some background information.
▶ For weddings you may need to ask the parents of the bride and groom for anecdotes and/or amusing events.
▶ At a business event you will need to research the topic and prepare your PowerPoint slides.

Begin by noting down the main points you want to get across. Planning your speech is a crucial part of your success as it can be fun and quite motivating. You have been asked to make a speech, so you should feel valued and take it as a compliment.

Don't allow nerves to put you off; instead, channel them as excitement. Use your creative energy to allay your fears and imagine your success. See yourself standing up on the stage or platform delivering your speech fluently. Do this as many times as possible before the event, as it will help you on the day.

Once you have done a little research, begin to get your ideas on paper or computer. At first your ideas may not flow freely, but you can always ask friends or colleagues to help you to get started. Sit quietly with a blank sheet of paper or a blank word processing document and just jot down anything that comes into your head. Don't be concerned if the words seem disjointed or vague. Thinking about the props, slides or photographs can also trigger ideas.

Start your speech with a strong opening such as a quote, and close with an equally strong ending for example a surprising fact. Memorize both so that the middle of the speech can flow without you being anxious about the first and final lines.

Decide the order of your speech and what points will follow on seamlessly from another. Find out what your audience already knows and make sure you do not cover areas they have heard before. Ask yourself the following:

1 How can I bring fresh information to my speech?
2 What would make the audience engage with my material?
3 How can I surprise them?
4 Who do I need to thank or introduce?
5 Where can I get the information I need?

Once you have written the bare bones of the speech, start to refine it. Decide on the main text and divide it into sections. Do not try to cram too much information into the speech. Select three key points and expand on those. Now is the time to go through your speech and to put in the pauses, spaces for audience interaction, and any stress on key words. Using different coloured pens or fonts will allow you to see clearly the key areas.

Once you have a final draft, time the speech exactly. Remember, there will sometimes be laughter, questions or applause. Never overrun your allotted time. Make sure you get people's names correct by noting them down before you speak. Be sure of your facts and check that information is accurate and up-to-date.

So, now you have your speech planned and prepared it is time to practise, practise, practise.

To start off with it is useful to rehearse in front of a mirror. You can see your general posture, gestures, facial expressions and body language. Notice all these areas and remember that all your movements need to be larger than usual in front of an audience. In a meeting room the same applies, except where there are fewer than 15 people.

When you have practised in front of a mirror a few times, try asking your friends or colleagues to give you some constructive feedback. Be prepared to listen and amend your speech, including non-verbal clues, according to the feedback.

Take some time to consider what to wear – the general rule is 'dress a little bit smarter than your audience'.

Whenever possible, be sure to check the venue in advance – the room and equipment. If you are using props, visuals, PowerPoint or slides, contact the venue to ensure that your room layout is exactly as you want it. If you have to use a microphone, it is a good idea to test it at least 15 minutes before the event. Everyone has a different tone to their voice, and the microphone needs to be adjusted every time.

Before you deliver your speech, breathe deeply and channel your nerves into excitement and enthusiasm. End on a high and leave your audience wanting more. Above all, enjoy yourself and your audience will too.

Introduction

This unique book will address some of the following questions:

▶ *Why is it that whenever I am asked to speak in public I avoid the situation at all costs?*
▶ *What happens to me when I go to interviews and face a panel of people? Why do I change from being a normal human being to a shaking wreck?*
▶ *Why does my forthcoming radio interview fill me with dread?*
▶ *Why do I feel sick at the thought of speaking at my best friend's wedding?*

These are just some of the questions I have heard as an executive and voice coach. You are already speaking in different situations to complete strangers on a daily basis. Anyone can develop these existing skills to deliver and present a memorable speech.

So what can this book do for you?

Chapters 1 to 3 will explain ways in which you can enhance your skills and learn new techniques of public speaking for a variety of occasions. You will gain tips on preparation, planning and organizing your speech. You will discover how to set clear objectives and will gain techniques to aid your delivery. You will begin to breathe correctly and use your voice to gain maximum impact. As you continue to tread the path of discovery you will understand how to connect and engage your audience. As your confidence grows you will be able to use silence and pauses effectively. There are also tips on using body language and gestures to bring your speech to life. For those of you looking to use a PowerPoint presentation or setting up a video conference, check out Chapter 4 for some helpful hints.

Chapters 5 to 22 concentrate on specific occasions and events, so you can choose which chapters best suit your needs. Perhaps you are looking for a suitable speech for a wedding or civil ceremony? Check out Chapter 5 for some interesting ideas. I have included some useful tips from a father of the bride (equally appropriate for the mother, too) who gave an excellent speech at both his daughters' weddings. All those speaking at weddings can find amusing ideas and quotes, as will those speaking at civil ceremonies.

Are you speaking at a sporting event or helping to raise funds for a local club? Chapters 10 and 14 are the places to look for further inspiration. After dinner speeches can be particularly daunting for the uninitiated so have a look at Chapter 9 for hints and tips.

You may be asked to speak at a funeral or a retirement party and you will find helpful quotes and toasts in Chapters 8 and 11 to give these events a special touch. There are specimen speeches taken from real occasions to encourage you to develop your own style. Just allow them to be your guide in what I am sure will be an exciting and rewarding journey.

Speaking in public may not always be at a large gathering or event. In your daily lives you have to speak to small groups on a variety of occasions. In today's society, 'networking' is a real buzz word as people attend a wide range of groups on a weekly or monthly basis. My clients have often asked me what they should say to a complete stranger at a networking event. They also ask about how to approach a small group who are deep in conversation without appearing rude. Find out how in Chapter 16.

Facing an interview unprepared can cost you the job. It may not always be those straight out of college or training who face the interview panel; very often people are asked to re-apply for their own jobs. Many people returning to work feel that they have forgotten skills and lost their confidence. In Chapter 18 you may find some of the ideas and examples helpful.

You may not think of speaking on the telephone as public speaking. However, for many people this is a very daunting experience and you will find helpful hints for a variety of situations including making an initial enquiry, being brief and focused, making a complaint and confronting authority.

Probably the easiest speech is when you can speak about what you know best – your hobbies or personal interests. Your enthusiasm shines through and your genuine interest carries the event by itself. In Chapter 15 you can have a look at how to improve on your knowledge and bring in comedy and the element of surprise.

There will always be stumbling blocks to overcome. It is useful to think about what may go wrong (see Chapter 28) so that you can be prepared. Technology may let you down, you may forget your notes or you may miss out a vital point. All these can be overcome; as with most things in life, they seem much worse at the time than they are in reality. To gain practice you may like to join a local speakers' club.

A few years ago when I was looking for a speakers' club in Brighton & Hove, I found nothing. After visiting a couple of Toastmasters speaking clubs in the neighbouring towns of Chichester and Guildford, I was delighted to find that the format really worked. The training they gave was excellent and just what my nerves needed. So, in 2001, after some months of research and publicity, I set up the Brighton & Hove Speakers' Club which chartered as a Toastmasters Club in the first year and currently has a vibrant membership.

If there is a speakers' club near you, give it a try. You are not expected to speak straight away and most clubs have a mentoring system to support newcomers. Just listening to others giving speeches can be motivating and entertaining. Speeches are evaluated, too, so that you can see where people have done well and where there is room for development. Then set a date for your first speech, it can be 60 seconds, two minutes or a choice from the manual.

If you can't join a club, try practising with a dictaphone or small tape recorder and play it back – this is a great technique.

Above all enjoy yourself – public speaking really can be fun and gives you a real buzz when it all comes together. I think speaking is rather like going on a holiday:

▶ *The journey needs careful preparation, organization and timing.*
▶ *You need to make sure you have everything arranged at your destination. When you arrive you feel a little nervous and apprehensive. However, when you settle down you really start to relax and enjoy yourself.*
▶ *You meet new people, gain experience and start to go with the flow. When the holiday is over you feel energized and know that – even if the hotel was on a building site and the disco kept you awake – next time, if you pay attention to the planning and details, it will definitely be better!*

Part one

From preparation to delivery

1

Plan, prepare and practise

In this chapter you will learn:
- *how to boost your skills and confidence*
- *how to determine speech objectives*
- *how to prepare and plan effectively*
- *how to order, consider and remember your content.*

So you've been asked to speak at a special event or give a zappy presentation.

What's your first reaction? Do your knees feel weak? Perhaps your stomach lurched at the very thought of standing up in front of a group of people? Well, you may be surprised to learn you are already doing it in a small way every day. It's easy enough to build on your public speaking skills and learn techniques to ease your fears.

Enhance your existing skills

Nearly every day you speak on the telephone. Admittedly, it's generally to one person at a time, but you have no script and no one to prompt you. It's automatic; you just speak with your own ideas and unique voice. Often you will pick up the phone and tell someone about an incident that has happened. You may chat about a recent holiday. Perhaps you need to arrange some business with a colleague. You don't give this a second thought despite it being a form of public speaking.

What about the public speaking you do in a face-to-face situation? The visit you make to the bank to arrange an overdraft or set up an account. The complaint you make to your local authority about a public service. The time you stood up and asked a question at a meeting. Did you write the script before you went? No, of course not. You trust your own ability to speak whatever the situation.

It is very encouraging to recall the times you speak to complete strangers without a script and without fear of getting it wrong. The skills you use on these occasions are the same. It makes no difference if you are speaking to small groups at meetings or larger groups at weddings. You already have all the tools you need to speak on those special occasions. With the help of this book you will begin to build on them and develop new skills and techniques. So don't panic – prepare.

One comforting thought is that you are the only person who knows what you are going to say. If you miss a couple of points you can always add them later; no one will know. If someone asks you to speak, take heart that others see you as someone interesting and are ready to listen to you. You may be chosen to speak as part of your job. Perhaps you are asked to deliver a speech at a wedding or family event. Although this is not quite the same as one-to-one it is still a great opportunity to hone your skills. Today, in all aspects of life, we are frequently asked to speak in public.

If you get to the heart of the matter by addressing the real problem of why you fear public speaking you will discover the real solution. This book also explains why just learning a few techniques will not help you unless you take a long look at what is blocking your way. The key is to boost your self-esteem and confidence, then you will be able to speak without fear. You will come to realize that you have the exact same value as those you will be speaking to.

One thing to help banish those butterflies is to make the decision not to panic but to prepare, plan and practise – the three Ps. Look at the case study below as an example:

Matt belonged to the local Lions Club and often helped to raise funds for the community. He was also active in organizing events and days out for the local youth club in his area. One day he was asked to give a speech at the regional Lions Club dinner and found himself feeling very anxious and afraid. Together we looked at his speaking experience and how he had used his powers of persuasion to raise funds and to speak to the young people in his care. He understood that he had been both confident and convincing when asking for donations. He felt motivated when he realized that he had spoken to large groups of unruly teenagers and succeeded in holding their attention. He began to realize that this experience could help him and he developed ways to build on this. He decided not to panic – but to plan, prepare and practise well.

Preparation

In getting started with your speech, first on your list is to determine the objectives. Then consider the timing and the make-up of your audience.

OBJECTIVES

What do you want your speech to achieve? Do you want to persuade, motivate, encourage, entertain or provide information? Sometimes it may be a combination of two or more. In Matt's case it was to provide some background information, thank a few people and to entertain. Decide what your objectives are and think carefully about what it is the audience need to hear. Matt needed to provide interesting information and decide what key points to emphasize. He also needed to build in some amusing stories and remember to thank particular people.

What follows are general guidelines for planning and organizing your speech. You will find further examples of planning for specific occasions later in the book.

Planning can be fun

If you like to plan with diagrams or pictures, take a large piece of paper (or use the computer) and draw a mind map or spider diagram. Plot your speech ideas and objectives so that you can see them clearly in front of you. Use coloured pens to highlight specific areas. You may need several thought maps or diagrams until you are satisfied that your speech contains all the vital elements.

If you prefer to plan with lists use the computer or a notebook to jot down your ideas. Then re-order them into the various sections of your speech.

Start with an introduction, then choose three key points to develop your main text and follow up with a conclusion. In all cases be sure to add in time for laughter, pauses, gestures and questions. You will find further information on structuring your content later in this chapter.

Insight

No need to panic, just prepare, plan and practise.

Timing

It is vital to ensure you do not overrun or be too brief and miss an opportunity.

If, for example, you only have 20 minutes for the speech or presentation, calculate: five minutes for the opening, ten for the main body and five for your conclusion or for questions if appropriate.

In a wedding speech where you are entertaining a group you may need to put in time for laughter and reactions. In a business presentation you may also have questions during the main body of your presentation. Speeches and presentations always take longer than when you practise them at home.

Insight

Remember that the audience's reaction, gestures and pauses need to be taken into consideration.

On all occasions it is very important to time yourself and each element of the speech. Try using a dictaphone or asking a friend or colleague to time you. If you are giving a business presentation this is vital as in most organizations time is money. Even at celebrations and special occasions people do not appreciate being made to listen for longer than necessary.

Once the preparation and planning is all in place the last of the three Ps remains – just practise, practise, practise.

Insight

Start with a bang, choose three points for your main text and end with a quote or startling fact.

Remembering your speech

So, you have prepared what you want to say but do you remember it all?

Here is a selection of techniques to help you remember what you have prepared.

You can:

▶ *memorize your entire speech word for word*
▶ *use a script and read your speech*
▶ *use notes and cards to jog your memory*
▶ *use visual aids*

▶ *use a combination of the above*
▶ *forget the notes and visuals and just be yourself.*

Let's have a look at all these methods in more detail.

MEMORIZING

Memorizing your speech is full of potholes. It is the one where you are most likely to lose your way and forget your lines. It will come across to your audience as stilted and does not allow for interaction. Usually it is rushed and chunks can be forgotten altogether. The time it takes to write it all out and memorize it, is hardly worth the effort. You are concentrating on getting the words out and not on the real meaning and impact. The result is never as good as other methods and is not advisable.

Insight
Trust in your own ability to remember, and you will.

READING

Reading can help a novice speaker to become more confident. There is a list of hints for reading your speech at the end of this section.

Insight
Five to ten minutes before you speak on any special occasion:

▶ *take a few deep breaths from the diaphragm*
▶ *focus your mind on the room*
▶ *look around with awareness and 'centre' yourself*
▶ *cut out the chatter and intrusive thoughts*
▶ *just 'be' for a few moments.*

Have you ever listened to someone reading a speech? How did it sound to you? Probably it was monotone and boring to the ear. Even if a speaker is good at looking up from the script, the eye contact is, at best, fleeting. There can be no real contact with the audience as your nose is glued to the script. If you as the speaker can read the speech, so can your audience. As a result they do not respond well to speeches that are read. It is obvious that the words are just being spoken with no real meaning or emphasis. If you listen to a natural speech there are pauses and asides. The speaker will respond to audience reaction. This is just not possible when it is read.

Sometimes, of course, speeches need to be read out in part if they include statistics or political statements. It is often the case that part of a speech can be read if the occasion demands, as in a court of law for example.

Also when you are learning how to speak in public, this is the way you gain confidence and practise.

So how can you avoid sounding stilted when you read your first speeches?

1 *Once you have written your speech say it out loud to someone and get feedback. Often you will write something and then when you hear it back it sounds too formal. You need to write in a conversational way so that it appears natural. Compare:*
   'I would like to emphasize how vitally important it is to fund this project. Please make a substantial donation to support this cause'
   with the conversational tone of:
   'I'm sure you all feel as passionately as I do that this is a worthy cause we'd all like to support. Let's show we care by giving generously.'
2 *Use a coloured pen to highlight words or phrases you want to stress or emphasize.*
3 *Use another pen to put in the pauses and time to look up at your audience.*
4 *Note where you will change your tone of voice to give vibrancy to your speech.*
5 *Double-space your text to add gestures and special points you want to emphasize or get reaction from.*
6 *Then practise with all these additions, pauses and notes so that you are as natural as possible.*

7 *If at all possible get someone to video you delivering your speech. Seeing yourself on camera is the best way to learn. Take notes and watch as if you were a member of the audience.*

8 *Now listen to your voice but don't watch. Make a note of all the vocal enhancements you need to make.*

9 *Then watch with the sound turned down. How do you come across visually? Make notes of changes you want to make.*

10 *Do a second video with the improvements and watch it with a trusted friend who will give you honest feedback.*

When putting your pages together, remember:

▶ *Make your pages easy to turn. Fasten them together so they cannot drop down or fall apart.*

▶ *Always number the pages.*

▶ *If you find it helpful you can use a coloured pen to divide the paragraphs.*

▶ *Do not let one sentence travel onto the next page.*

▶ *Put pauses in just before you turn the page.*

Using these tips you will be able to read your speech more fluently and with greater impact. Eventually you will be able to move on to the next method.

USING NOTES AND CARDS

This is the second best way to deliver a speech that does not require visual aids (for example, overheads or a PowerPoint presentation).

Insight

When using notes, remember to number them and attach them with a ring at one corner to avoid dropping them.

The greatest advantage is that you maintain contact with your audience. The speech is there in note form and you have a useful memory aid. You are able to make eye contact and your delivery

is natural and flowing. Index cards work best with key points
on each card. It is not advisable to use A4 sheets of paper as
these rustle and can fall out of your hand. When using index
cards remember:

1 *Decide how many cards you want – three to six is usually
  enough.*
2 *Put down a maximum of three main ideas on the cards for
  each section. A) Your introduction, B) the body of text, and
  C) your conclusion. (Use larger writing that is easy to read but
  not capitals.)*
3 *Number the cards and join them with a ring (easy to turn over).*
4 *Put diagrams, quotes or figures on separate cards and slot
  them in where needed.*
5 *If you are speaking at a lectern – move away and use different
  parts of the floor or stage. (You can take your notes or leave
  them behind – practise doing both.)*
6 *When you feel confident start moving away from the lectern
  without notes and weave in gestures too.*
7 *Trust yourself to remember and don't refer to your notes too
  often (practise)!*
8 *Picture in your mind the points where you will move, pause
  and change pace.*

USING VISUAL AIDS AND OVERHEADS

Using a flip chart can be very helpful for you and your audience.
The great advantage is you can prepare it in advance. You can
be inventive and use colours, pictures or diagrams to bring your
speech alive. Many speakers also use flip charts to note down
audience responses or ideas during an interactive presentation.

For the novice speaker a flip chart can be used for a speech on
almost any topic. It serves as a great memory aid and visual
stimulus. You can start by writing up headings for each part of
your speech – one heading plus three sub-headings for each page –
then as you go through turn the page over. If you are a keen
gardener, for example, you can also bring in slides, or pictures

and display them. You can draw diagrams to refer to, and make use of props such as small plants and seedlings.

In this example your main heading may be:

How to prepare your garden

With sub-headings of:

Introduction

Digging and weeding

Preparing the beds

Choosing your plants

Conclusion

If you know your subject well further headings may not be necessary. If not, then additional sub-headings under each section could be added. Three is usually a good number to aim for.

It is important to keep the visuals uncluttered. As a guide use no more than about four lines per visual and no more than six words a line. If you are making a list, again about four lines down is enough. Make sure the top heading grabs the attention and describes the main topic you are introducing. Be consistent and use the same colour, font and text size when using charts, slides and PowerPoints.

A COMBINATION OF METHODS

When you are starting out on the public speaking road it is useful to begin by reading your speech. The three Ps are vitally important, as this is how you will improve your speaking style. Then slowly progress to using cards and bullet points as you get more confident. Using a combination is the bridge to success.

When you feel comfortable using notes, start to cut them down to bullet points only. You will still be reading but there will not be full sentences; this takes practice. Follow the methods above for the cards but use full pages, more sub-headings and keep them on the lectern. Slide one page to the side as you go. You will notice that with less text you will begin to connect with the audience. You will be able to raise your eyes from the text more often. You can add a gesture or two and experience what that feels like. Taking your hand off the lectern, raising your eyes and trusting your notes goes a long way towards the final stage of public speaking.

NO NOTES, NO VISUALS – JUST YOU

What is it that allows some speakers to speak at every occasion with no notes or aids? Do they really stand up there and deliver with no practice or preparation? Yes and no.

In order to be that confident you need to have had some practice or personal experience of speaking in public. Most will have done a job that involved addressing people on a regular basis. It is seldom or never the case that a truly effective and inspirational speaker is able to just get up and speak. Some people appear to be spontaneous but in reality they may have adapted an old speech to 'fit' the new occasion. In the toastmaster's speaking clubs people get practice in impromptu speaking. They learn how to speak about any topic for about two to three minutes with only a few second's notice. This takes a great deal of practice and not many can really 'hold' an audience from the beginning and sustain it.

So does this mean that you will not be able to speak without notes? Absolutely not. After you have used some of the methods above you will begin to gain confidence in your delivery. You will present speeches that begin to flow and you will start to feel comfortable as you take the floor.

Insight

It's like learning to drive, eventually it becomes automatic and you will begin to be relaxed and spontaneous.

When starting out the best way is to read your speech, then move to small index cards when you become more confident.

Start to believe you can

One very useful tip is to recognize that as soon as you believe you can deliver without notes, you will be able to. It is all about *trusting in your own ability*. Just trust that all will be well and you will deliver in your own natural style. It is not advisable to copy someone else.

Insight
Watching successful speakers can be very beneficial but remain true to your own style.

Start to visualize yourself giving the speech without notes. Hear the audience applauding your success. Practise giving yourself these positive affirmations to eliminate the negative self-speak. These statements may not be true just yet but by repeating them you are enhancing your self-belief and boosting your confidence. This is a useful tool and you will begin to feel more confident and fluent when speaking.

Get into the habit of repeating these mantras daily before an important speech:

I am able to speak without notes.

I can deliver this speech fluently.

I am a confident speaker.

I trust my own ability and preparation.

I am ready to speak naturally in my own style.

Audience

It is helpful to know as much about your audience as possible. This gives you the upper hand when faced with questions or interruptions. In the case study earlier, Matt asked the committee chair for a list of the members who would be at the dinner and what information they already had. It was useful for him to know that most of the members were not aware of the information he was going to impart. This resulted in him having the element of surprise.

Find out what your audience knows about your subject. If you are giving a speech about a completely new topic for them, be prepared to provide additional background information. If your audience is known to you, for example at a birthday celebration, then find amusing anecdotes or stories to entertain the person you are speaking about.

WIIFT

Ask yourself **What's In It For Them,** in other words what the audience is coming to hear and what they want to take away from your speech. If the audience is looking for a particular piece of information they will expect to hear it. If you are speaking at a celebration, people want to have fun and discover something interesting about the person they are toasting.

When speaking at a celebration try to find out as much as possible from friends and relations about the person in question. At a wedding I attended recently the best man had prepared several amusing photos of the groom. He had then stuck them on the underside of a few strategically placed chairs. During his speech he asked some guests to remove the photos and show them to the audience. This involved the audience in the speech and proved a huge success. Think about ways you can do the same and invite the audience to participate.

If you are addressing an unfamiliar audience (say, a small group of between five and 20 people) a way to involve them is to personalize a small prop that illustrates a particular point. A colleague who was a financial advisor gave a presentation at a local networking group. He started his speech by tearing up a five-pound note and exclaiming, 'So this is the way you treat your money!' Most people remembered his presentation long after the event.

Another example is a presentation given by the local florist. She didn't try to sell the products or arrangements, instead she brought along some flowers. During the meeting she put them together expertly as she spoke about the events she was preparing for. It was colourful, visually stimulating and made a real impact.

Content and organization

You have now timed and prepared your ideas. You have decided how you will remember your text and the methods you will use. You have also considered your audience and their needs. Depending on the length of your speech you now need to organize the various elements into a logical sequence. There will always be:

- ▶ *an introduction*
- ▶ *a main body*
- ▶ *a conclusion.*

Also, if possible, a silver thread that runs throughout the speech making it easy for your audience to listen to. As you move from one step to the next give your audience a signpost. Only you know what you are going to say and when you are listening to a speech it is difficult to focus when there are no signposts.

One way of organizing your speech ideas is to use images or pictures. You can create a chain of ideas using pictures, for example, the branches of a tree, using lines from a central point. Place your central ideas on each branch and then add further branches as you add further points. As a result you can use the pictures to memorize the chain of events or points.

As you draw the picture you can clearly see where more ideas are needed and where to cut down. You can also use just one image for your chain, as in the example below.

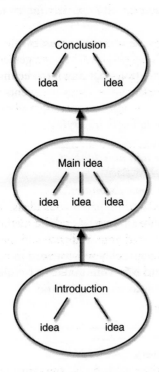

Draw simple pictures that will remind you of what you want to say. For example, if your topic is 'Global Warming', you may put some ideas on your diagram such as research findings, polar ice, water levels, flooding, climate change and so on. Now order the sequence of these ideas logically in the chain.

Another example is a speech at a birthday celebration. After you have introduced yourself, you may decide to tell a story about the person whose birthday it is. Use the chain of images to jog your memory. After the story you could say, 'So now I'd like to tell you a little about how that story illustrates (Jo Bloggs's) character.' For your sequence of ideas you can use phrases such as:

'Now I'd like to move on to...'

'Finally I am so pleased/happy/delighted to say that...'

'So everyone please raise your glasses to...'

In a more formal situation after any introductions that are necessary you may use:

'Firstly I'd like to begin by saying...'

'Moving on we will now look at...'

'Let's consider some examples...'

'In conclusion/To sum up...'

Obviously you will replace these with your own words. Not only does this silver thread help your audience to follow where you are going but it helps you to stay focused too.

Openers and closers

How do you make an audience sit up and take notice? The first 60 seconds of any speech or presentation is crucial. You will be judged even before you open your mouth.

(**Note:** In the section on 'Creating your personal image' in Chapter 2 you will find tips on what not to wear.)

As Winston Churchill said, one of the best ways to control your nerves and be spontaneous is to prepare effectively. He had a rule that for every minute of his speech he needed to prepare for one hour.

SO, WHAT MAKES A GOOD OPENER?

Questions

Start with a question – especially for a club presentation where the material is somewhat dry. Emma, who works for a local charity, likes the idea of starting with a hypothetical question. She says that this gets the audience's attention and involves them from the outset. For example, 'Do you know how much money the club has managed to raise over the past 12 months? Well, I think you'll be surprised…' Obviously the audience she is talking to are aware of the subject matter and are able to give her a reasonable guess.

More suitable for a wedding speech would be, 'So, as father of the bride I'd like to ask those of you who know my daughter, what do you think was her greatest achievement?' Of course, you don't have to wait for the answer, as you don't wish to be interrupted, just pause and then say, 'Well I'm sure that you will be amazed when I tell you that it was…'

Facts

Start (and/or close) with a stunning fact or a surprise statement about your topic, something others will be unlikely to know. For example, when giving a speech to persuade people that a pedestrian crossing is vital in a village street, you could introduce a startling fact, 'Last year five people died and 22 were injured crossing this road – that's a rise of 60 per cent on the last two years.'

Metaphors

Or start with a metaphor. Metaphors can be a real solution to that all-important opening. It is something unexpected and replaces the blindingly obvious. They are surprising; they conjure up images and appeal to emotions. When you link them effectively to your main message they can be a real winner.

If your charity/club has not performed well and you are delivering bad news, try using this 'flying' metaphor to ease the pain of your team, 'I was on a flight recently and there was a great deal of turbulence as we came through the clouds. My companion remarked that this was the way he was feeling about an up and coming interview, rather shaky and feeling sick! This made me realize that you are probably feeling the current turbulence as much as I am. Despite not receiving the expected funds this year we can still aim for a safe landing if we all pull together over the next 12 months.'

It is important to determine the pain your particular group is experiencing, for example:

▶ *resistance to change*
▶ *lack of funding for a club*
▶ *sadness at a funeral.*

Of course metaphors aren't just used for presenting a problem. Metaphors can liven up any speech and can be used for many different occasions. For example at a birthday party a friend could say of the birthday girl, 'She sometimes reminds me of a small dog. She needs to exercise often, she drinks plenty of liquid and she responds well to people giving her instructions. She easily runs for a couple of miles and she flops down at your feet at the end of a day with her tongue hanging out!'

You get the picture!

LEAVE THEM WANTING MORE

Close with a strong statement or reveal a startling or amusing fact.

For the best man
'Finally, I'd like to leave you with this: James (the groom) has recently been given the Toastmasters award for Competent Communicator. On the cricket pitch he was a lousy batsman and he couldn't play football to save his life. It seems in public speaking, however, he is a master. Over to you James!'

Closing formal speeches or presentations

Any of the tips above apply, but for a formal speech on, for example, change management, you may include an interesting quote such as, 'Every change is not an improvement, but every improvement needs change.'

Your conclusion needs to serve as a review of your message or key points. Summarize the main points, refer to the purpose and then end with a relevant anecdote or quote. Remember that this is your last chance to leave an impression. Your final words will carry your message. Try using a prop to finish with. For example, in a presentation on how funds were raised for a youth hostel, Tom concluded, 'So, this year we are looking to top that great achievement by asking you to dig deep.' He then produced a spade from behind the curtain and mimed digging on the stage. He ended with the words, 'Come on everyone let's dig down and beat last year's donations, if I can do it you can!' He got loud applause and the result he was looking for.

COPING WITH THE Q & A SESSION THAT FALLS FLAT

So, you end your speech with a great final phrase and then open the floor for a question and answer session. Everyone is enthusiastic and then the final question you ask 'Anyone else? No... OK, so that's it then.'

Somehow it all peters out and you are left standing there.

Top tip

At all costs, keep a closing sentence for after the questions so that you can go off to resounding applause.

Room layout and equipment

Part of your planning involves the room layout and the availability of props, technical equipment or screens. You will need to prepare any handouts, props or visual aids you may want to use. If possible, it is always a good idea to visit the room where you will be speaking. Stand in the exact spot to get a feel for the atmosphere and where your props and equipment are going to be. If this is not possible make sure the room layout is exactly as you like it and all the equipment is available. If you do not know the venue give them a quick call in advance. On many occasions, you will still have to re-arrange furniture and locate equipment on arrival despite phoning ahead.

Room layouts vary and it is useful to consider what will work best for you *and* your audience.

- ▶ *Will you be using a lectern or standing behind a table?*
- ▶ *Will you be on a stage or platform?*
- ▶ *Where will your audience be seated?*
- ▶ *How many seats will be needed?*
- ▶ *How will they be seated (at round tables, in a horseshoe, in a meeting or theatre style)?*
- ▶ *What kind of lighting will there be in the room?*

Before speaking, call the venue to enquire about all of the above as this is an essential part of the planning process.

2

Speaking and presenting skills

In this chapter you will learn:
- *how to breathe correctly*
- *about pauses and silence*
- *how to be heard clearly*
- *how to cut negative chatter*
- *to create your personal image.*

Breath control

In order to develop your own distinctive voice you need to find it!

If you are tense, your voice will be too. If your breathing is shallow your voice will not project or sound confident. Your vocal cords can be greatly improved by exercising them correctly, as most singers are aware. No singer would perform without first doing vocal exercises. So, speakers need to do the same with their most important tool – the voice.

If you breathe correctly from the diaphragm this will get rid of the jitters and the wobbly feelings. This kind of breathing counteracts the panic you feel and allows the body to relax. You can train yourself to respond to fear, not with tension but with relaxation. The diaphragm is located at the bottom of your ribcage. Place your hands on your diaphragm with the fingers facing each other. You will feel a little space at the bottom of your ribcage.

Insight

If you remember to pause and breathe during your speech, you will:

▶ *calm your nerves*
▶ *deliver more confidently*
▶ *aid your memory.*

BREATHING EXERCISE

Slump back in your chair. Let everything go. Let your arms hang down and your legs stretch out. Breathe out and sigh or make a noise if you feel like it. Slowly relax all your muscles from the head, through the body, down your legs and to your feet. If anywhere is tense, try to let go of the tension. Let your jaw relax and feel the throat muscles relaxing too.

Yawn and stretch for a moment. As you yawn feel and relax the throat and neck. Be aware of the breath as you release it and notice the sound as you go 'Aaaah'.

Breathe in deeply from the diaphragm the second time and go 'Aaaah' as you let the breath out. This is a really useful exercise as you are letting all the stale air out and then breathing the fresh air into your lungs.

Then slowly sit up in a relaxed state.

Stand up and place your hands on your diaphragm and inhale – let the diaphragm expand, don't force it up just let air expand into your lungs and push your stomach out. Exhale and let the muscles contract. Breathing can be through the nose or the mouth, whichever is the most comfortable. Be careful not to move the shoulders or chest muscles. Now do this five times. Practise this exercise on a regular basis, as it will help you to project your voice to the back of the room when speaking or presenting.

Before speaking to any audience, making a telephone call or going to a meeting, get into the habit of breathing like this five times. Not only will you become calmer, you will also give your brain a boost of oxygen enabling clarity of thought. This is vital before speaking on any special occasion.

RELAXATION EXERCISE

Try slumping in a chair and letting out all your breath.

Hang your arms loosely by your sides and allow all your muscles to relax as you lean forward to an upright posture. (Retain just enough muscle strength to keep yourself from falling over!)

Drop your jaw onto your chest and let your mouth hang open gently.

Relax the facial muscles.

Allow your body to curl forwards slowly as far as is comfortable.

Then curl very slowly and gently back to an upright position.

Stay relaxed with your chin now on a level and your shoulders down.

Breathe deeply and repeat.

Note: If you feel dizzy, remain upright and continue breathing.

Insight
The more natural and relaxed you appear, the better people will listen to you.

Pauses and silence

Being comfortable with silence is one of the speaker's great assets. All those ums and ahs can be reduced if you are able to 'be' with the silence. All audiences need to absorb what you have said. Unlike you, they have not heard this speech before and need time to think. Next time you practise your speech record it and notice how many ums and ahs you have. Next time see if you can just repeat the sentence and pause where the ums and ahs were inserted. The audience will have time to think and so will you. Your speech will appear measured and unflustered. In addition, one of the greatest tools for getting attention and creating suspense, is the use of pausing and silence.

Insight
Create suspense by pausing for a little longer before key points.

Imagine if Martin Luther King had continued straight after 'I have a dream ...' But of course he didn't. He paused and let the impact of his words really sink in. That's one of the reasons why everyone remembers his speech to this day. People were hanging on his words and wanting to hear what this dream would be.

Here are some other examples:

At a wedding:
'Welcome guests. I know three things about the groom that I just have to tell you ...' If you pause after this statement, look around and smile to yourself, you will create tension and interest. People will listen to hear what you are going to say next. If, however, you just carry on with no pause, this suspense will not be created and the words will lose their impact.

At a business meeting:
'I have come here today bearing very good news' ... (pause, breathe) ...

Again the pause heightens the tension and the breath allows you to enhance your delivery.

'... I can tell you that we succeeded in beating last year's target by ... (pause, breathe) ... £2,000.'

Silence can be created when you are really looking for dramatic impact. If, for example, you are telling a story to illustrate a point, you may need to move around a large stage or platform. Similarly, you may want to allow people to see and understand a flip chart or PowerPoint presentation.

An informative speech:
You are giving a speech about the life of a person who had achieved a particular goal against all the odds. You have come to the end of the first half of the story with, '... he had certainly not been expecting what was to come next ...' silence. Walk closer to your audience and look around at their faces. You may make a gesture at this point or shake your head in disbelief; whatever seems appropriate for this situation. The silence creates the tension, then you resume your speech.

A fund-raising review:
You are giving a PowerPoint presentation on the results of this year's fund-raising events. You have presented four slides in fairly quick succession. People have had to take in a lot of information. You put up a slide, which summarizes the main points. Now you have two options:

1 *Talk them through the slide point by point* or
2 *Create a silence where you introduce the slide. Allow time for everyone to read it through and make their own notes. Then briefly go through the points facing the audience.*

It is very frustrating for people when no time is given to take in what has been said. Many people like visuals but need a few minutes silence to reflect and note down any points they need.

At the end, ask questions to ensure everyone has understood and is taking away the information they need.

Insight

Focusing on areas of your speech that you feel a connection to will inspire your audience.

Your voice

Everyone has a different voice. It is unique to you and not one person sounds the way you do. Isn't that special? Sometimes families have similar voices but they are never identical. You have a voice fingerprint. Your voice touches people in your own special way and that is one of the keys to your success. You may be saying: 'But my voice is too quiet' or 'I speak too fast' or 'My voice is too high and squeaky.' Yes, it's true, you may need to work on voice tone and quality. You may need to project more and use effective breathing techniques. These are all areas that can be enhanced and improved. Your particular unique voice is an essential part of the whole speaking process.

You don't have to be loud to put your point across successfully. With a little adjustment your voice can carry to the back of a room despite the soft tones.

Your body needs to be in alignment. It is not possible to project your voice with your chin on your chest. You get your best vocal performance when you stand upright.

POSTURE AND VOCAL ADJUSTMENT

▶ *Relax and get your weight evenly distributed.*
▶ *Place your feet about ten centimetres apart.*
▶ *Take in a controlled supply of breath from the diaphragm before speaking. (This calms the nerves and sends oxygen to the brain – which you need!)*

- *Emphasize the strong consonants, particularly at the end of words.*
- *Stay focused, looking towards your audience.*
- *Pay attention to effective word formation and lip movement.*
- *Work on your own sounds so you can project your voice and fill a space effectively.*

You do not need to be a performer or a showman/woman. Most speakers are better just being natural when they speak. If you speak from the heart and really mean what you say, your audience will follow you. If you connect with your audience and stay calm by pausing and breathing, you will pull them along with you. They need to breathe too. When you are explaining something interesting or new, they need time to absorb it. We often forget that this information is new to our audience, unlike ourselves who have (PPP) planned, prepared and practised it for weeks.

DICTION AND PROJECTION EXERCISE

In order to project your voice you need good breathing, relaxation and confidence.

Try this exercise in a secluded space. It can really help.

Stand at the back of the room and look at a point on the opposite wall. Imagine you are speaking to it. Stand with your feet a little apart and with your shoulders down and relaxed. Keep your chin level and your throat free. Say the following, being clear to pronounce the consonants (these are not 'A E I O U' – which are the vowels).

'Ship ahoy!' 'Help Help!' 'Look out!' 'Stand back!'

Say them one after the other and bounce the sound off the wall in front of you. Now put your hands on your diaphragm, breathe deeply out–in–out–in. Then repeat the phrases again. Remember to expand the diaphragm (feel your ribcage expand outwards) and keep the mouth and throat relaxed and open. The sound should be low and mellow, not high and forced.

Now on one breath (breathe in) try the vowels... A...E...I...O...U.

Make them hit the wall. If you are out of breath then you need to practise your breathing exercises. The muscles of the diaphragm are like your fingers when you start to play the piano – stiff and unfamiliar with the new position. With practice you will be able to project and breathe with ease.

Now put your vocal ability into an exercise to practise every day.

Think about your breathing and don't forget to pause and allow the words to flow naturally. Allow yourself to exclaim, concentrating on the vowels this time.

> *'Oh what!' 'No!' 'Well!' 'Really!' 'Oh heavens!' 'You can't be serious!'*

This is meant to be exploring your vocal variety and to be fun as well. Now repeat the consonants: 'Ship ahoy!' 'Help Help!' 'Look out!' 'Stand back!'

Ideally do this in front of a mirror to check if you are really opening your mouth and breathing correctly. This needs to be done in a relaxed position so you may like to begin with the breathing and relaxation exercise first.

CARING FOR YOUR VOICE

A word of caution. If you intend to speak on a regular basis take care of your vocal cords. Your vocal cords are tiny light flaps of tissue that can get easily damaged. After speaking have a period of silence to allow them to recover. Drink tepid water during your speech. Humming is a good vocal exercise and can free up vocal cords when mucus is a problem. Avoid clearing your throat loudly as this also damages the vocal cords if done frequently.

If you feel any tightness in your voice or it begins to hurt, pause, take a sip of water and then resume. If you are running an all-day workshop or seminar, always avoid speaking at length to people during the breaks. Instead, take time out for your voice to recover by walking outside to get some fresh air if possible. If not find a quiet area where you can gather your thoughts. Breathe deeply and give your vocal cords a well-earned rest.

Insight

Every singer does vocal exercises before they sing; so should every speaker before they speak.

Gestures

The very best way to make an impact on your audience is to be as natural as possible. Gestures can add great value to a performance but they need to be sincere and really appropriate for the occasion. It is important to be authentic as audiences can pick up on gestures that do not align with the true message of the speaker.

To make gestures effective, remember:

▶ *Make the gesture suit the words.*
▶ *Feel the gesture, don't just do it.*
▶ *Make the gestures bigger than usual – make them convincing.*
▶ *Smooth well-timed gestures have more impact.*

Think about what gestures you make naturally. Fear can drive you to keep your hands in your pockets or clasped at your front. Relax your hands by shaking them gently before a speech. Keep them loosely at your side even if this feels strange at first. Think about your audience and how you are going to help or inform them. Focus on your message and the pressure about how you look will be diminished.

Top tip

Good planning and preparation will enable you to create fluid gestures. Put time aside to think about where your gestures will be most appropriate. Use them sparingly for greater impact.

So, the best way to appear relaxed and in control is to:

1 *Use PPP.*
2 *Be certain of what you are going to say and do, and when.*
3 *Breathe and use pauses.*

As a result, making off the cuff remarks or interacting with the audience will be a breeze. Think about a joke or a story you have told many times. How much have you embellished it or changed it over the years? You probably know it so well it is easy to re-tell it in any way you like and with various gestures. It's no different when you're speaking on special occasions. However, keep your speed of delivery a little slower than your normal conversation. This gives the audience time to follow your speech. Then practise. The more practice you get, the more connection and rapport you will create with your listeners.

Cut the chatter

You can decide which thoughts you allow to occupy your mind. To a large extent you determine your own speaking path by the thoughts and emotions you choose to accept or discard. This is often hard to come to terms with. Sometimes it is a challenge to change patterns of behaviour you have drifted through life with. You feel comfortable with them, they are 'old friends' and although they may be bad for you, you hang on to them, staying in your own comfort zone.

So how can you turn out the old chatter that no longer serves you: 'I'll dry up', 'I'll make a fool of myself', 'I've never been able to speak in public', and start to introduce the new images and thoughts?

CREATING NEW HABITS

Be patient. If you are patient and replace the old chatter with: 'I'll give this a try', 'Everyone makes mistakes', 'I'll learn as I go', you will slowly begin to trust yourself. You will suddenly become aware that you *do* have control over what success you have in the future by what you pay attention to in the present.

Refuse to be concerned with regrets and guilt feelings; tell yourself that fear will be replaced with quiet confidence. Fear is only possible without knowledge and trust in your abilities. Look at those times when you have been successful, remember them and shut out the voices that tell you: 'You will fail', 'You can't do this', 'You're no good', 'What if they laugh at you.'

Instead replace your old chatter with positive messages. Make the old voices laughable and take on the new ones. No one is like you or has *your* stories to tell. You may think that what you have to say is not interesting but everyone has experiences that interest others. Try answering these questions:

▶ *What do I bring to this occasion?*
  (e.g. an interesting story, knowledge to share, a useful piece of information)

▶ *What am I leaving behind?*
  (e.g. bad weather, unhelpful chatter, the terrible traffic)

▶ *What are my expectations at this event?*
  (e.g. do I want to be right/faultless or do I want to enjoy the moment and give my best?)

▶ *What can I tell myself now so that this day/occasion is special?*

GETTING CENTRED

Five to ten minutes before you speak on any special occasion, remember:

▶ *Take a few deep breaths from the diaphragm (base of the ribcage).*
▶ *Focus your mind on the room.*

- *Look around with awareness and 'centre' yourself.*
- *Cut out the chatter and intrusive thoughts.*
- *Breathe and just 'be' for a few moments.*

Colin had received very negative feedback years ago which affected his confidence. He was asked to present a report to the whole class, and his hands began to sweat and he felt physically sick. It didn't help when he was told to 'get on with it' and not to be 'so stupid'.

This had a very damaging effect on him as, after several similar experiences, he felt he really was 'stupid' and of course he had, in his mind, plenty of evidence to prove this. As time went on he gained more self-respect but always had these 'voices' in his head. As a result he found he was not able to assert himself in day-to-day situations and avoided conflict. After joining a local speakers club and receiving coaching to boost his confidence he realized that the 'evidence' proving his 'stupidity' was no longer there. He could see that he could in fact be a very able speaker.

He was delighted to relate a very positive experience some time later. He had been into his local insurance office and confronted the manager who had made a mistake on his policy. He put his case across in a very convincing fashion and got the result he was looking for. He is now more able to face his fears and work through the barriers to effective communication.

Make a concerted effort to put the past and all its negative experiences behind you. Be aware that you *can* change the patterns and give yourself a chance to speak on those special occasions if you choose to. Invest some time on the techniques in this book and see the results for yourself.

Creating your personal image

No matter whether you are speaking at a family wedding or at an international conference, you will be judged as soon as you stand up to speak. Think about the occasions when you have met people for the first time. You noticed their appearance and their attitude. You may have had thoughts about the way they were dressed or if they had nice eyes. You made unconscious judgements about them before they even spoke a word.

Before you speak, think about the mood you want to create. Will it be relaxed and informal, or will you be giving a powerful sales presentation? You can send out very different messages with subtle variances in the way you dress. It is useful to consider that most of the time you will be viewed from a distance. If you stand in front of your mirror you will have a totally different image of yourself.

Try standing in front of your mirror in the outfit you will be wearing, complete with any accessories. Then stand back as far away as the audience will be. Notice if your style has the same impact.

CHOOSING YOUR COLOURS

A colleague told this story at a recent conference where she had presented.

'I dressed in a smart suit as I was presenting to the Law Society. However, I wanted to add a touch of colour, so I wore a bright red shirt with a high collar under my jacket. After the presentation I was told that this had 'shone' in the lights and had actually distracted the audience from my message. I realized that I had not taken into account the impact that the red shirt had from a distance or under the bright lights.'

On this occasion red earrings and a strong red necklace may have been a better choice. On a man a smart suit with a brightly coloured tie may have the same result.

Colour can add a dash of energy and excitement to a speech. Don't be afraid to use it but think carefully about the impact each item will have. If you wear a strongly patterned tie, suit or blouse it may look great close up but can easily distract at a distance. For a formal setting, darker plain colours are usually more effective. You do not want to take the attention away from your message. In a less formal setting, lighter colours can be worn but stick to plain materials or very subtle patterns.

SHOWING YOUR AUTHORITY

This will depend on the occasion and the mood you want to create.

In a formal setting, women will be more authoritative when:

▶ *wearing a suit either with trousers or a skirt to the knee*
▶ *choosing long straight skirts of a darker shade and a plain material*
▶ *selecting blouses that are more formal where the cleavage is not too apparent*
▶ *wearing high heels to create authority*
▶ *wearing hair up to create a more sophisticated look.*

In a more informal setting it may be more appropriate to:

▶ *leave your blouse open at the neck and your jacket undone*
▶ *wear jewellery that can add sparkle and a dash of colour (keep it very simple for a formal setting).*

Men will appear more formal when:

▶ *wearing a dark blue, black or pinstriped suit as is usual in the business world*
▶ *choosing a brown or grey suit for slightly less formal occasions.*

For an informal occasion it may be more appropriate to:

▶ *select a smart/casual jacket and trousers*
▶ *wear a lightly striped or patterned shirt (plain may be better for more formal occasions)*
▶ *wear plain or subtly patterned ties (or no tie).*

Top tip

Remember, your upright confident posture is your main asset when speaking on a stage or platform.

CONSIDERING YOUR ENVIRONMENT

Top tip

If possible visit the room where you will be presenting. It would be a disaster if you arrived in a dark blue suit and the main decorations were also dark blue. You do not want to fade into the background. If it is not possible to view the room in advance take a coloured scarf or two sets of jewellery if you are a woman. If you are a man, it is advisable to take two suits and a couple of ties.

William, the president of a speakers' club told of the day he won the UK International Speakers Competition.

'I went into the room the day before to have a look around. I noticed the heavy light grey curtains, the grey chairs and the lovely pale blue carpet. Upstairs on my bed I had laid out my smart, medium grey suit with a pale blue shirt and light grey tie. I was at a loss as this was the only suit I had taken. Luckily, my colleague was the same size as me and had come to give me moral support. He had brought a suit for the evening dance, which was dark blue and looked fine with my blue shirt. He kindly offered to lend it to me for the competition. If I had worn mine I would not have stood out at all from my surroundings. After that I always took a spare suit when I was speaking at dinners and competitions.'

CASE STUDY

GETTING IT JUST RIGHT

A good rule of thumb is to dress just a little smarter than your audience. For example, if most people are in open-necked shirts or blouses and no jackets, slip on a jacket for your speech and take it off when mingling afterwards. Add touches of colour to a formal suit to create an element of surprise but avoid loud statements that will detract from your delivery. You want to be remembered for what your words conveyed not for a fashion statement.

If you respect your audience by dressing well, creating rapport will be easier. Your image speaks volumes and it only takes a little time to consider how you come across. This is always time well spent.

Top tip

If you don't have a long mirror, invest in one. As a public speaker you'll definitely need it!

Another concern speakers have is about being too tall or too short. Shorter women have the advantage of high heels but men can also buy blocked shoes to increase height. However, it is not really that important. If you stand tall and exude confidence you will not need heels as your attitude will carry you through. If you are tall, celebrate the fact and avoid stooping or leaning forward.

3

Writing a great speech

In this chapter you will learn:
- *how to come up with speech ideas and formats*
- *how to use language effectively*
- *about the benefits of alliteration and onomatopoeia*
- *the value of 'people' words.*

Content is all around you

Ideas for writing a speech are all around you. You will think of topics in the shower, waiting for a train, and in unexpected places. Carry a pad around with you to note down ideas and amusing incidents to weave into your speeches. The best ideas are always those where you have had personal experience: situations that give you a real buzz and ideas that excite you and make you want to tell people. Even the kind of things that you chat about to your friends can turn into a speech. If you are captivated by an idea you become a better speaker and you will motivate your audience. People like to listen to a speaker who has strong feelings about a topic. They may disagree with your arguments but will respect your passion and enthusiasm. Families and friends can be a rich source of material for your speech. What unusual hobbies or jobs do they have?

Alan, who attends a London speakers' group, decided to become a
monk in his youth but then he fell in love with a nun and realized
his destiny lay elsewhere. Another member told of her desire to
swim the Channel and the resulting speech was full of interesting
events leading up to the swim.

Do you get on your soapbox? Everyone has a theme they like to
bring to the table. Perhaps yours is music downloads, politics or the
behaviour of teenagers today. Try making it into an inspiring theme
to impress your audience. Radio and television are good sources
of topics too. Listen to the news and see if something grabs your
attention. Talk shows can be a mine of information and often trigger
a reaction or deep-seated emotion which thus stimulates a speech idea.

After watching a television programme on adoption one speaker told
of her own search for her birth parents. She had never thought of
speaking about it before but the programme gave her the confidence
to speak out. The speech was so personal and her feelings so genuine
that she got a fantastic reaction from the audience that night.

Another powerful speech was from someone who had heard about
a daring rescue on the radio. This story prompted him to speak
about his time in the fire service. He told of some amazing rescues
he and his colleagues had been involved in.

Format and structure

Now that you have found your topics or speech ideas what do you do?

1 *Write them all down in no particular order. Or select pictures
  to represent ideas.*

2 *Take a look at them and decide which ones grab your imagination the most. Make a list of two or three.*

3 *Then write down all the words and phrases that come to mind around one of the topics.*

4 *Do the same with the others, using just short words and phrases at this stage.*

5 *Decide which topic is your favourite and really jumps out at you. Write this at the top of a clean page. Continue to write all the ideas around this topic that come to mind. Include all viewpoints and opinions, using short bullet points at this stage.*

6 *Then find the three or four main points that best support your own ideas. List these ideas in order of importance or relevance.*

7 *Now put the meat onto those main ideas – opinions, stories, anecdotes, amusing incidents, quotes and so on.*

8 *Decide in which order you will deliver your points and sub points. Colour code them for a visual aid.*

9 *Then write your introduction, your main text and your conclusion or summary.*

10 *Write the outline of your speech using small cards for the main points and sub points.*

11 *Decide on your final quote or end phrase. Memorize the first few lines of your speech and the last two.*

12 *Practise, practise and then practise again.*

If you are presenting material as part of your job try to colour the speech with the passion of your own experience. Once again, use stories to illustrate facts and dry material where you can.

For all speeches you need to develop a theme that will run throughout. Decide what you want the audience to go away with. Do you want to inform or amuse or both? Ensure you have a good construction with a clear beginning, middle and end. Work though the above points to help you plan.

Insight
Make your thoughts and ideas an easy path to follow for your audience.

Now that you have the 'how' of your speech you need to consider language and texture. Keep things simple – this is a useful rule but just how simple is also worth thinking through. Some of the best speeches are woven with colourful vocabulary. People who play with words in the form of alliteration or onomatopoeic phrases also enrich their speeches.

Alliteration

This is the use of words using the same sound at the beginning of each word. For example, if you were giving a speech on your holiday and describing the sun going down you could say, 'It was an amazing sunset that slowly dropped behind the palm trees.' If you used alliteration you could say, 'It was a beautiful sunset that bathed the palm trees with a brilliance that was breathtaking.'

If you were describing a concert you had been to you might say, 'The music was wonderful and lifted my spirits.' If you used alliteration you might say, 'The music struck me with soft soothing sonatas that strengthened my soul.'

Obviously, alliteration is not always appropriate and would be heavy if repeated throughout the speech. However, used wisely it can give great colour and depth to your delivery. It is particularly useful for description and to liven up dull material.

This is a good example from a technical speech: 'I am about to bore you with building regulations. They are relevant, rigorous and robust. They relate to the recent redevelopment in Richmond, so let's rock and roll!' This caused a laugh, created instant rapport with the audience and got everyone's attention.

> **Insight**
> Making your speech sound effective with a variety of language
> will enhance the impact.

Onomatopoeia

This imitates the sound that the word represents. Some examples are: hiss, thud, pitter-patter, whisper, hoot and so on. Again, the use of these words can enliven your speech and have a positive impact on your audience. They are particularly useful when describing an action.

'The horses clip clopped along the cobbled street', this evokes the sound in people's imaginations and allows them to 'hear' what you are describing. Another example is, 'As we walked along the shore the sand crunched under our feet and we could hear the waves swishing across our path.'

Using different kinds of descriptive language helps people to imagine the scene you are talking about. It invites them into your world and helps them connect with your message.

If you are speaking about your neighbour and you say, 'My neighbour is grumpy', the message is clear but how much more impact would it have if you said, 'My neighbour is a really cantankerous old grump.'

Giving a wedding speech you may mention the bride's dress and say, 'What a beautiful dress Emma is wearing today.' However, you have not said what was beautiful about it, it is just a common remark made at any wedding. Try, 'Emma's dress really shimmered in the sunlight' or 'The dress Emma wore today was a celebration in satin and silk.'

The human-interest element

So how do you substitute those abstract words for the ones that will really engage your audience? Here is an example:

> **'The outcome of this research is that overall sales are above average.'**

In this case the information is accurate but there are no people involved. Your audience wants to hear about people, then they can relate better to your information. You need to search for the human-interest element. Who are getting above average results, the sales team, the PR department? So, why not change the words around and say, 'This research shows that our sales team are getting above average sales overall.'

If you probe a little further you will find that more people were involved. Who did the research? Who benefits from this information? Who do the sales team sell to? Now it is becoming an interesting human story rather than dull facts. 'Our researchers discovered that the sales team were delivering our latest laptops to PC Global like hot cakes – we are impressed.'

Insight
If possible, tell real stories to illustrate your key points.

Top tip
The next time you prepare a speech think about the words, the way they sound, what they mean and how you can craft them. Use them to convince, amuse and inspire. This will make your message even more vital and appealing.

4

....

Technology and props

In this chapter you will learn:
* *how to access information on the web*
* *about effective props and visual equipment*
* *tips and techniques to aid the technical process*
* *about potential pitfalls.*

Information collection and verification

Using the web to check facts and collate information is now commonplace. Where in the past we would have reached for an encyclopaedia, we can now trawl through the internet. Some of the best websites for general information include:

▶ *www.wikipedia.com – probably the biggest multilingual free-content encyclopaedia on the internet*
▶ *www.infoplease.com – an online almanac*
▶ *www.britannica.com – full text of* Encyclopaedia Britannica
▶ *www.Encyclopedia.com – more concise information*
▶ *www.biography.com – 25,000 articles on current and historical figures*
▶ *www.yourdictionary.com – thesauri with foreign and English language dictionaries.*

Props

Props can greatly enhance a speech. They can also detract from the message so they need to be chosen carefully. Imagine yourself in the audience. Ask yourself what kind of visual aid would complement your message.

If you are presenting a speech at a family celebration, for example, think about what amusing props would enliven your speech. If the speech is about motivating your club members to contribute to a charity event, think about what props would add to the impact.

Prepare the props so you do not need to turn your back when presenting them to your audience. A small table at the side is best, so that you can access them easily. If you want the element of surprise, cover them with a cloth or place them in a bag. The most important thing to remember is that they need to be easily to hand.

Top tip
Never turn your back to your audience or you'll lose the momentum.

If you are using several props make sure they are in the right order. You can either colour code them or number them in advance. Less is more, so it is not advisable to have more than three props in a speech lasting under one hour. Always make sure they are relevant to the topic of your speech.

Insight
Remember: props are powerful and aid perception. They enable you to pause, involve the audience and create instant rapport.

Visual equipment

HANDOUTS

The most common visuals are handouts. These are often used when numbers or facts are included in your speech and are given out at the end as a summary. It is not advisable to give your audience a handout while you are speaking. This will detract from your words and discourage your audience from paying attention to your message.

Some examples of handout visuals are: diagrams, graphs, pie charts, spider diagrams, cartoons and pictures. The advantage of a handout is that the audience has a reminder of what they heard to take away with them. This is particularly useful when the subject matter is a little dry.

POWERPOINT

Slides and overhead projectors are now used infrequently. The PowerPoint presentation has taken over and can greatly enhance a speech – or kill it!

Here are some tips when using PowerPoint presentations:

1 *Use images to reinforce numeric data.*
2 *Summarize the key message at the top of the slide.*
3 *Leave plenty of white space on each slide.*
4 *Use bullet points not complete sentences – less is more.*
5 *Alternate colours on tables to improve visibility.*
6 *The message is more important than your logo/name.*
7 *Keep your logo/name in the same place on each slide.*
8 *Keep each slide to a minimum of three points.*
9 *Increase attention with full screen images.*
10 *Keep fonts and overall design consistent.*

11 *Use either photos or clip art – not both.*
12 *Tell a story with a beginning, middle and logical conclusion.*
13 *Space out your information for a smooth professional presentation.*
14 *The image they will take home is your last one – make it the best.*

There are some great resources for including amusing slides to enhance your PowerPoint presentations. Web generators let you create, produce or generate something. For example, you can upload a photo and then change it into a pencil sketch. On another website you can key in a quote or a signature and transform it into any script you fancy. You can even copy text onto an image of your choice. For example, if your presentation was part of a course in conflict management, you could copy and paste key phrases onto a hammer flying through the air. If you were speaking about a recent holiday, you could paste words or phrases onto a ship or plane.

Visit the following website and have some fun: <u>www.redkid. net/generator/bumper</u>. There are many more so just put 'web generator' into your browser and see what comes up. One or two funny slides can really make a difference to a dull presentation. Obviously too many can kill it so keep a balance and enjoy.

Insight
Why not experiment with a web generator to enhance your slides?

FLIP CHART

This is a great visual aid. Speakers use them to add spontaneous drawings or diagrams to emphasize a point. Just keep the following in mind:

- ▸ *Use thick blue or black pens.*
- ▸ *Write large letters/diagrams – ideally not capitals.*
- ▸ *Make sure there is plenty of white space.*
- ▸ *Do not crowd the sheets with information.*
- ▸ *Bullet points are clear and easy to read.*

If you can prepare these sheets in advance – all the better. Then you will not have to turn your back. Asking someone in the group to write things up for you is another way to get around this.

Insight

Using a flip chart? Always write in large (lower case) letters using black or blue ink.

Interaction

If you tell a story, even factual information can be entertaining. Think of the situations around your facts. What story can you weave into the dry material to sweep your audience along with you? How can you get your audience involved? Nothing surpasses interaction as a way to engage, teach or persuade listeners. Ask hypothetical questions such as: 'Do you know how much money you need to invest per year until you retire so that you can live comfortably?' or 'Have you ever thought about what you might do if the British Isles became on average ten per cent cooler?'

Top tip

Asking questions (not necessarily needing an answer) helps to engage your audience and gets them thinking.

Pitfalls

Avoid common pitfalls by remembering the following:

1 *Always check your equipment and any hired items at least one hour before you begin the setting up process.*
2 *Setting up always takes longer than you expect so plan in advance.*
3 *Make sure you have a contact at your venue who knows the equipment.*

4 *If the PowerPoint presentation doesn't work, check the*
   following (as obvious as they seem, each one is vital):
   ▷ *Did you use the correct sequence when turning on the*
     equipment?
   ▷ *Are both the laptop and the projector turned on and*
     plugged in?
   ▷ *Have you put in the correct password (if necessary)?*
   ▷ *If you are using a memory stick – is it inserted correctly?*
   ▷ *Has the cap been removed from the projector?*
   ▷ *Is the screen placed so that the image can be projected*
     effectively?
   ▷ *If the image is too small, move the projector further back*
     from the screen. If too large, move it towards the screen.
   ▷ *If the image is slanted, adjust the feet/foot on the*
     underside of the projector.
   ▷ *If the image is too low – place a book underneath the*
     projector. If too high, use a lower table or adjust the foot
     on the underside of the projector.
   ▷ *If using a remote control make sure it is attached*
     correctly and that the slot is not loose.

Do not be afraid to ask for technical help in advance. You do not
want to have to stop in the middle of your presentation if it goes
wrong.

Insight
Check through your equipment before you depart, when you
arrive and just before you start.

Microphones

Most speakers prefer to speak without a microphone but it is
common where large audiences are expected. Be aware that
microphones can be temperamental and need checking and
re-checking before the event. Avoid banging the mike to see
if it works or blowing into it, as this can cause damage.

Instead, just say 'testing' a couple of times and get the technician to adjust the levels for you. Have a small signal that tells the technician to raise or lower the levels.

Never speak with your lips on the mike as this muffles the sound. Hold a handheld mike just below your mouth and speak normally. When turning your head move the mike as you speak unless it is fixed. Make sure that when you make a gesture or show a prop your face is not too far from the mike. The best way to do this is to pause when making the movement so your words are not lost.

Most annoying for an audience is when the speaker has pages of notes rustling into the mike. Put your notes on cards that are easily laid on the lectern and do not rustle. Once again, when turning the page/card, pause for a moment before you speak.

Oh, and remember, if you have a mike, it's surprising how many speakers forget to turn it on before speaking!

Speaking into a microphone can be helpful to an audience. It is definitely worth learning how to do it efficiently for maximum impact.

10 THINGS TO REMEMBER

1 *Decide on your speech objectives, e.g. to inform, motivate or entertain. Then research your key areas and make a plan with key points to emphasize.*

2 *Include a strong beginning, main text and punchy ending.*

3 *Establish the length and timing of your speech. Remember to build in pauses and audience reactions.*

4 *Practise your speech and get feedback.*

5 *If possible, visit the room where you will be presenting. Check all names, key facts, equipment and props.*

6 *People come to see you, so use PowerPoint as a prop only. Keep slides and handouts concise with plenty of white space. And remember to use a consistent font.*

7 *Vary your voice tone and pace. Also work on your projection and diction. If you stop in the middle of your speech, breathe, pause and start again.*

8 *Place props in front of you. Face the front and speak out to your audience.*

9 *Use eye contact and engage your audience with a question or two.*

10 *Think about a visual that would enhance your speech. Then introduce it to make full impact. For example, you might decide to make the final image the most memorable.*

Part two

Speaking at major 'life' events

5

Weddings/civil ceremonies

In this chapter you will learn:
- *how to plan and write your wedding speech*
- *the benefits of adapting sample speeches*
- *how to deliver with impact.*

In the UK we have, up until recently, leaned towards weddings where certain things are done to follow set traditions. Today, because people tend to travel more, weddings are influenced by other trends outside our own country. Foreign cultures are becoming more a part of our daily lives and weddings are held in a wide variety of buildings, not just in a church or registry office. This has a direct influence on who speaks at weddings and also on the content of speeches.

In addition, many marriages sadly end in divorce but, surprisingly perhaps, many people marry again. This will also have an influence on the content of speeches.

If you are getting married for the second or third time, it is likely that one of your children may give you away. Other members of your family may also act as the best man or woman. In today's society the mother of the bride is just as likely to give a speech as the father. In fact anyone close to the couple can be asked to speak. Weddings can be very formal occasions or quite informal family celebrations.

If you choose the more traditional route then there are certain formalities that need to be taken into consideration. If you want to have the bride's father and/or mother, the bridegroom and the best man/woman making speeches then timing will be important. Also, some planning of the content will be essential so that they are not repeating information. It is not uncommon for speeches to overrun and this can be very boring for those listening. Ask everyone to keep their speech to under ten minutes. If there are more than three speeches, under five minutes is advisable. This way you can ensure your audience does not fall asleep!

If you have been asked to speak, how can you make your speech memorable? What impression do you want your wedding guests to go away with? How do you write a speech you can be proud of?

An entertaining wedding speech

The first question to ask yourself is: 'How can I best entertain the audience while keeping to the traditional thanks, congratulations, and toasts?'

For a wedding or civil ceremony this will most likely be a mixture of thanks plus some amusing or interesting incidents.

The speech is never about you and who you are. It is always about the people whose wedding you are celebrating and the audience. In a wedding speech the focus is on the couple and their interests. This takes the pressure off you, as people will be focusing on your stories and less on how you look or speak.

By the time the speeches are announced most people have had a couple of drinks and are happy to laugh and get involved. You, however, need to be sober!

Everyone in the audience wants to be relaxed and in a mood of celebration. If you deliver your speech feeling relaxed and happy then your audience will mirror your attitude.

When planning your speech you may want to include some happy memories or personal stories about the couple/individual. You may know of an amusing side to them that others haven't heard. When adding humour be mindful of causing embarrassment and be aware of the feelings of others.

Insight

At a wedding people like to be entertained. Start with a joke and end on a quote is a good mantra.

METAPHORS AND ANECDOTES

Metaphors based on the hobbies or interests of the recipient can add spice to a speech. For example in this speech from a father of the bride: 'My daughter rides through life as if she is showjumping. She is fearless, always pushing herself and the horse to greater heights. Still, she's learnt how to pick herself up after a fall – she's had several along the way. But, look at the results now. In achieving her degree she's jumped the highest hurdle of all and stayed in the saddle!'

Other examples of anecdotes you can adapt for wedding speeches include the following:

Overheard at a recent stag night: 'Well, I didn't know the bra size of my fiancée but she had asked me to buy her some sexy underwear. I said to the assistant, 'I guess the bra would be about thirteen inches.' She told me that it would be most unusual and that the size was more likely to be 34 or 36 inches. 'Well,' I said, 'my head size is six and a half inches so I reckon it would be about two cricket cap sizes.' She thought I was joking but I was serious. I showed her the cap as I had taken it with me.

'Guess what? I wasn't far out after all. Apparently it's the cup (in my case cap!) size you need!'

To start your speech try: 'A good wedding speech should be like a mini skirt – short enough to be interesting but long enough to cover the subject. So here goes.'

'Preparing a speech for a wedding is like strong coffee – very stimulating but impossible to sleep after. So, it wasn't the wine or the coffee that made my heart thump at two a.m. last night, the thought of this speech did – it's still thumping but… here goes!'

Deliver with impact

YOUR SPEAKING IMAGE

You are judged even before you stand up or begin your delivery. People are quick to pick up on the way you walk and carry yourself. They will notice your clothes and style of hair. If you look confident then they will relax. If you are nervous this will affect their mood too. In order to make a good first impression you will have spent time on the way you look. At a wedding, even if it is not a formal occasion, you need to look smart and neatly dressed. You will walk to the centre with a firm step or stand up at the table with confidence. Even if you are wobbling inside and your hands are sweating, there's no need to show the audience how you feel.

Top tip

Turn your nervous energy into enthusiasm for your speech. Create a 'fizzy spot' just where you are standing and feel the 'fizz' rising up through your body creating energy and vitality.

Focus your attention on others to relieve stress.

If the focus is on you these questions will arise:

- *How will I appear?*
- *How can I remember my script?*
- *What will they think of me?*
- *Will I dry up and look a fool?*

However, if the focus is on them the following questions arise:

- *What personal gems and facts can I give them?*
- *What props will I need?*
- *How can I involve key people?*
- *Who do I need to thank or mention?*
- *How can I ensure they go away feeling happy and included?*

If you plan, prepare and practise (PPP) you will deliver a great speech that people will remember for years afterwards.

Insight
Stay sober before your speech – your friends will thank you.

_____

Speech PPPs

PLANNING

It is useful to have a rule of three. Three objectives, three points for each.

For example:

- *Introduction – Childhood story with a picture, an anecdote and an amusing prop.*
- *Main body of text – Three events in the person's life or characteristics relevant to the occasion with or without props.*
- *Conclusion – Amusing story of an incident in the adult life of the person plus a toast to the couple or partnership.*

Respect the feelings and sensitivity of others when preparing jokes and anecdotes.

PREPARATION

These points are helpful for anyone giving a speech at a wedding or civil ceremony.

1 *Note down all the hobbies and interests of the person you are speaking about.*
2 *Pick out some you think may be amusing or interesting for the invited guests.*
3 *Ask the family/friends for any amusing incidents in the life of the person.*
4 *Think of the props/pictures/stories around these incidents to show/tell during your speech.*
5 *Order your speech into a clear beginning, middle and end.*
6 *Decide in what order your points will flow best for each section.*
7 *Decide where to bring in props/pictures and mark this clearly on your copy of the speech.*
8 *If you need to refer to other people or to thank them, make a list of their names.*
9 *Pick out specific areas to make them feel special (pretty dress, great hairdo, etc.)*
10 *Be upbeat and positive; avoid jokes and embarrassing remarks.*

PRACTISE

In order to be relaxed on the day you need to practise your speech regularly before the event. If you leave it until the last minute you will be setting yourself up for failure. All good speakers practise, even if it appears they don't.

It can be useful to speak in front of a mirror, record onto an audio tape or even video yourself to see how you come across. Alternatively, you can ask a friend or family member to give you feedback.

Tips for practice and delivery

1 *Write out your speech in full with notes on use of props and pictures.*
2 *Put in the pauses, gestures and actions if relevant.*
3 *Make sure the introduction, main body and conclusion are clear.*
4 *Record the speech on a small tape recorder or video camera and listen to/watch your delivery.*
5 *Make any amendments, additions or deletions.*
6 *Record the speech again until you are satisfied with the result.*
7 *Listen to the tape as often as possible so that you become familiar with your speech. Use the props and make the gestures as you listen.*
8 *If you need to have notes then put the main points onto three small cards to hold in your hand. Join them with looped clips so they don't fall on the floor.*
9 *Never read from your full script as you will lose your place if you look up and it will sound boring.*
10 *Smile and keep eye contact with the guests by picking out friendly faces.*
11 *Stand tall, keep your throat free and relaxed and your shoulders down.*
12 *Breathe and remember to pause before the key points.*

It's OK to feel nervous. Everyone gets nervous so channel your nerves into excitement. Feel the buzz of the room and allow it to give you a boost of energy. Take several deep breaths before you begin and remember that everyone wants this to be a successful day so they're on your side. Take a sip of water, breathe, pause, look around, smile and then hit them with your first line.

Guidelines

All weddings will vary according to the formality of the occasion and religious beliefs. Speeches will also vary and so everyone will have their own ideas on how these should be conducted. The structure below acts as a guideline and there is further information before each sample speech.

Insight
A wedding speech should be short and sharp with sizzle.

The order for speeches at a traditional wedding is as follows:

1 *The bride's father (or mother or close relative) gives a speech and proposes a toast to the couple getting married.*
2 *The groom will then reply to the toast and give his prepared speech followed by thanks and a toast to the bridesmaids/maids of honour.*
3 *The best man gives his speech and replies on behalf of the bridesmaids/maids of honour.*

Insight
Everyone feels nervous, so channel those nerves into energy and excitement.

Father of the bride

Top tips for the father of the bride or male relative:

▶ *Start out with some good points about the occasion.*
▶ *Thank everyone for coming particularly those from far away or abroad.*
▶ *Mention grandparents and absent friends or relations.*
▶ *Praise your wife on how she looks and/or those who were the organizers.*
▶ *Make a few amusing comments about the preparation.*
▶ *Praise your daughter and mention some brief incidents in her life.*
▶ *Talk about your son-in-law and bring in some amusing comments.*
▶ *Mention the guests and how wonderful they look.*
▶ *Raise a toast to the bride and groom.*

FATHER OF THE BRIDE SAMPLE SPEECH 1

Kindly contributed by John Postlethwaite.

Hello and welcome to everyone on this wonderful (joyous, special, happy) occasion. A special welcome to the four grandmas who have an average age of 88 years. My mother is 95 and still beats me on the daily crossword.

(The underlying principle here is to talk up the occasion and single out particular popular people for mention with the intention of making everyone feel comfortable and happy. After a few drinks and with plenty of pauses to encourage cheering this is not difficult.)

At the other end of the life's divide a special welcome to my grand nephew James, age six weeks. Welcome also to guests from overseas (mentioning them by name and country) and not least to Tom and Sarah who have actually made the supreme sacrifice of getting here on the M25.

If you enjoy your day then thanks are of course due to the head of Mission Control – Rosemary (mother of the bride), and doesn't she look good. But, if the horse kicks your car or the marquee collapses then blame me (turning to son-in-law to be) and that is how it is going to be from now on!

It is of course my happy role to tell you about Emma (bride), and doesn't she look absolutely stunning today! She has been a model daughter and I can prove it (project or hold up picture of her as child model, or indeed try to highlight any particular achievement).

Emma has always been a lucky girl, lucky in work, school, friends (nod towards her friends), love (nod to the bridegroom) and of course, her parents.

(Here list exploits and accomplishments such as education, travel, sport, work, and family history repeating itself etc.)

After I first met John (the bridegroom) and it was clear his intentions were serious (and that he had a very good income) I said to Emma 'But you can't possibly marry this man, he's too good looking, he's devoted to sport, he works all hours and he drinks too much!' 'But', said Emma, 'YOU married mother!'

(Try to finish on a light hearted and/or sentimental note, perhaps recalling a special family peculiarity or incident. End the speech by toasting the bride and groom.)

Please enjoy the day and the rest of the speeches, and join me now in raising your glasses to the bride and groom – to Emma and John.

FATHER OF THE BRIDE SAMPLE SPEECH 2

Written by the author.

Well, despite all the nervous moments, here we are on the big day – didn't they do well. The ceremony was so moving and the song that Martina sang for us really touched my heart so a big 'thank you' to her. The black and white theme worked well didn't it? Everyone made an effort and I have never seen so many shades of white – amazing.

Before raising a toast to the wonderful bride and groom I would like to thank everyone for coming today. Particularly those who braved the M1, the M25 and the various airport delays. Still, you all made it I am glad to report and we are particularly grateful to Jean and Fred who have travelled from Spain to be here today. I would especially like to mention Grandma Fiske who looks magnificent in her flowing black dress and white feathered hat. We are all very proud of her and know that she has contributed a great deal of time on the table decorations – thank you Grandma.

We are sorry that our great friends from Scotland Liz and Paul were not able to be with us today but they have sent a wonderful gift and their very best wishes to all.

(Further comments or amusing incidents can be added about the various people you mention.)

I know that my wife has had a lot to do over the past months, planning and organizing. This is a role where she is totally at home. Unfortunately, I have had to do the fetching and carrying and this is a role where I am not so at home. I think I've lost about 18 pounds which can't be all bad. However, we got there in the end and it has all been worth the effort. Today my duty is to make sure you all enjoy yourselves so any fights breaking out or unruly behaviour from the under 15s – see me!

So on to my daughter Petra who was very unruly at the age of 15. Now, as I see her sitting here in her beautiful gown and flowing veil, I have to say her mother and I are very proud of her. She has achieved so much in her life from her first prize for her art in college to her latest exhibition of paintings in London. We were told that 'arty' children would always be a problem but this has not been the case at all and we are delighted at her success. She will know that her nickname is 'Mona' after the famous painting and today she really lives up to that name.

Joe will be a really caring son-in-law as we have already seen how much of a support he has been for Petra. We have shared many amusing moments but I will not embarrass him by mentioning them here. Suffice to say that he has a wicked sense of humour particularly after a glass of wine or two.

To everyone here I would like to say what a stunning crowd you look in your finery and of course to the finest of them all – please everyone stand, raise your glasses and wish health, wealth and happiness to the bride and groom – Petra and Joe.

Mother of the bride

Below you will find an example of a wedding speech for the mother of the bride. There are many examples of wedding speeches on the internet but none for the mother of the bride. These days it really can be any relative or friend who makes a speech and this gives flexibility to the occasion. You can adapt this speech to suit and add in your own stories and events.

MOTHER OF THE BRIDE SAMPLE SPEECH

Kindly contributed by Marian Way.

Hello everyone.

(She starts by giving a little background to how she came up with ideas and her research for the wedding day. She involves the audience by asking them a question to start her speech.)

Do you like my frock? (She could have inserted a story of the frock and where she found it.) I went on the internet for some help with my speech. I typed in 'mother of the bride speech' but there weren't any tips for mothers of brides – only hundreds of sites selling mother-of-the-bride outfits. It seems that I am supposed to just be decorative. (Pause and smile.) But, as it's the only day in my life I will be mother of the bride, I thought I'd make the most of it by giving a speech as well as wearing a nice frock.

I mean, I have to make the most of being mother of the bride today. (Look around and pause.) Tomorrow I will be a mother-in-law.

A few weeks ago, we were watching one of those property programmes on TV, and the presenter remarked that a particular home was extremely autobiographical. Now, I don't know about you but I thought an autobiography was a book – not a house – so that took a bit of thinking about. I came to the conclusion that he meant that you could tell a lot about the owners from being in the house – a bit like the old 'Through the Keyhole' programme with Lloyd Grossman: (Pause take on the accent and deep voice) And who lives in a house like this?

(This was a good idea – linking back to a TV programme that everyone could relate to.)

These days many houses are very individual, and do reveal something about the personalities of the people who live in them.

I got to thinking that the same can be said of weddings. There are the standard things people have – white dress, hotel reception, honeymoon in the Bahamas – and you can even buy a package deal in some hotels, with the MC, the table plan, flower arrangements and honeymoon suite all thrown in. Or, you can have a very different wedding. X was telling me about her friend's son who married on a beach on a Scottish Isle and the marquee and everything had to be brought over by boat. And someone else told me about a wedding in a cave in Cornwall where the guests had to wear hard hats.

But, I think we are somewhere between the two. You haven't had to arrive by boat or wear a hard hat, but I don't think this wedding could be described as 'standard' either. In fact, the more I think about it, the more I reckon the word 'autobiographical' sums up what we have here today.

So who has a wedding like this?

(Good idea to repeat this question in the form of the TV title.)

Let's start with sunflowers. Who in their right mind would choose to ask several of the guests to grow the flowers for the reception? And then wait with baited breath throughout the summer to see whether they'd come up, and if so, at exactly the right time, and in sufficient quantities?

(Hypothetical questions to involve the audience.)

And yet that's what we did, and even though we had to buy in a few extras from the florist at the last moment, it has given us

a lot to talk about throughout the summer and, I'm sure, today – and there are several people in this room who can now claim to be experts at growing sunflowers.

(Once again she involves the audience.)

I want to take this opportunity to say 'thank you' to everyone who took part in this rather wonderful experiment. And, if you've been wondering about the table names, they are all kinds of sunflowers.

(Great personal touches here to interest family and friends.)

Then we move on to dresses. Not for my daughter the standard white – or cream – dress. When we turned a corner at a wedding fair we were visiting and saw a dream of a dress in emerald green, we both knew that she would be dressed in emerald green today. I want to thank X, on our behalf, for the wonderful work she has done in creating all the dresses for today. I think we can safely say there's no other wedding with dresses like these!

Our photographer is another friend – and he too has taken his role seriously, coming all the way from Gloucestershire to spend a day with us looking at suitable spots for the pictures.

There are lots more features of this wedding day that are 'autobiographical' – Y's tiara, the Buddy Holly music, the cakes, the hog roast, the men's socks – each has a tale to tell, and if you want to know the stories behind these features, you can ask us about them later.

Right now, I want us to acknowledge all the time we – and all our helpers – have spent planning – and looking forward to – today. For the last 12 months, we have all been living in expectation of today, counting the days, and working together to make this dream wedding a reality. And if you think about it we've spent that year ensuring that today we'll be making lots of memories that we can re-live in the years to come. So, a year looking forward and many years looking back. But the only way we can make sure we have memories to re-live is to really LIVE today. To be present in the here and now, not thinking about yesterday or tomorrow. To enjoy the surroundings, talk to each other, dance, eat, drink, and be merry.

So let's drink to that! To being here, now.

(She ends with a lovely toast.)

One very strong element of this speech is the very personal autobiographical theme running through it. This is a unique family event and of course yours will be too. Just add the same personal stories. Ask yourself what makes this day unique to our family? Bring it alive with anecdotes and stories. Capture the special personalities who will be involved. If you tell it from the heart your audience will be swept along by your enthusiasm.

___

Groom

Top tips for the groom. He will usually:
- ▶ *Thank his mother- or father-in-law for the toast.*
- ▶ *Thank them for their daughter, for the reception and for being welcomed into the family.*
- ▶ *Mention some amusing or interesting anecdotes about how he met his wife/partner.*
- ▶ *Tell a couple of short amusing stories.*
- ▶ *Thank the guests for coming, particularly those from far away.*
- ▶ *Thank the guests for their gifts.*
- ▶ *Thank the best man or woman, bridesmaids, pageboys, maids of honour and ushers.*

It is also a tradition in the UK to present the latter (and sometimes both sets of parents) with small gifts. The groom usually raises a toast to the bridesmaids or maids of honour.

GROOM SAMPLE SPEECH

Contributed by Michelle McManus.

Below you will find an example of a groom's speech. (**Note:** The following speeches were taken from actual weddings.) The groom is marrying a woman who has a young son, Fred, by her first marriage.

I would like to thank my mother-in-law for her wonderful speech and her toast to enjoying the here and now – I agree.

As many of you will know I am a shy retiring type that likes to keep quiet and take my time about things, therefore you can understand my nervousness at standing here before you and making a speech. (Pause.) I have been fearful of this for weeks and as you can imagine it isn't the first time today I have raised myself from a warm seat with paper in my hand... (Pause).

When I was younger I always pictured myself marring a beautiful woman, getting a house and possibly children, but as relationships and years (pause) 45 to be exact, came and went, (slowly) I felt that dream slipping away.

So what did I do? (Look around at your friends and relations and pause.)

Well, I inserted an 'ad' in the classified 'wife wanted' and the next day hundreds of letters arrived with the same reply – have mine! So, that's how I got Clare. (Wait for the laughter – give them time.)

Seriously though, I am very lucky Clare has made my dream come true not just by becoming my beautiful wife but for also sharing Fred with me. Who would have thought all my dreams coming true in one day. (Look at your wife.)

I am also very lucky to be sharing this dream with you, our friends and family. Thank you for coming, especially those who have travelled so far to be here today and for your gifts and well wishes.

(Look at the specific people you mention as you thank them.)

I will never forget the day Clare and myself first met.

Fifteen years ago I was in my veterinary surgery preparing for my next patient when I turned around and saw this beautiful bird, chest pumped out, looking helpless and in need of my touch. Then I noticed Clare holding the seagull and from that moment I knew Clare was the one and I held a torch for her for the next 11 years. There were a lot of house calls to see to her sick greyhounds during that time too.

Four years ago Clare and I finally became a couple. They say what's worth having is worth waiting for. Clare, you and Fred were definitely worth the wait. (Look at your wife and her child.)

When I finally plucked up the courage to propose I became scared, so scared in fact I began to shake and went pale, but not quite as bad as I was today. I went and bought the engagement ring and thought of all the different ways I could propose. Christmas was coming and I thought, great, I'll do it then. (Long pause to create suspense.)

One night just before Christmas we were talking about presents and I just happened to mention that Clare may have a special present this year. Well, Clare nagged me and nagged me until I got up in the middle of the night in my boxers and went to the boot of the car where I had hidden the ring. I returned to the house before getting arrested and you've guessed (pause) I asked Clare to be my wife.

Thank you Clare for becoming my lovely bride.

(Then turn to Fred.) Fred thank you for being my best man, you are doing a great job. Well, I have to say that, his speech is next and I know he will be ace.

Fred and I have grown to be good mates over the last few years, often referring our relationship to Gorillas. Gorillas have packs.

The youngest being a Black Back, the middle a Brown Back and the eldest a Silver Back. Well Fred, yesterday you were the youngest. It will be a long while before you become a Silver Back like me but today you made the Brown Back – I'm proud of you.

Thank you to the young ladies who have done such a great job in helping Clare up the aisle today, although I hope she came to the Church of her own free will! Also, the ushers did a great job so please raise your glasses to Lottie, Olivia, David and Domino.

I'd like to thank the parents, Mum and Dad, for being so patient while waiting for me to finally get a bride. Thanks also for your love and support over the years.

To all our guests I would like to thank you for coming, particularly Hannah and Frederick for braving the rough English Channel. Many thanks to all of you for your wonderful gifts displayed over there, they look fantastic.

Finally thank you to Clare's parents for those kind words. Do you remember? It began with 'Well son, I feel sorry for you...' and [Mum's name] for all those lovely puddings you send back with us when we visit. You said Clare isn't a brilliant cook so I took your hint and bought her this. (Hold up a large cookery book.)

Well I hope you all enjoy today as much as my Wife and I will and please raise your glasses ladies and gentlemen to the bridesmaids and my beautiful wife – Clare.

Best man/woman

Top tips for the best man/woman:

▶ *Thank the groom for the speech and for the bridesmaids'/pageboys' gifts etc.*
▶ *Add some spice and humour to the occasion.*
▶ *Include some stories about the groom.*
▶ *Prepare some props to enliven the stories.*

- Stories and funny incidents are great but beware of embarrassing the couple or their relatives.
- Raise a toast for absent friends and any e-mails and cards from them can be read out.

BEST MAN SAMPLE SPEECH 1

Contributed by Michelle McManus.

(Boy aged 11, the son of the bride.)

Thank you Sean for your toast to the bridesmaids and for their lovely gifts and of course for mine! Thank you, Olivia and Lottie for making such beautiful bridesmaids. David and Domino were also great ushers.

On the subject of beauty, Mum you look a million dollars, I'm very proud of you.

And I am not the only one who thinks that. Sean, you look like the cat that has just got the cream and of course (pause) you got me as a bonus!

Of course Sean you look fab too, a bit of spit and polish does wonders for anyone. As the man of the house when Mum met Sean I was naturally concerned. You know, making sure he was good enough for my mum. Over time I saw he made my mum happy and if my mum is happy, I am happy. But Sean I hope you will remember that I am still the man of the house! (Pause for laughter.)

When they announced their engagement I became a little uncertain. Uncertain about names and what to call you Sean so I'll just call you 'Pop' if that's OK.

Along with Sean comes a name change, and names, don't you agree, are so important.

Take Sean for example. His name means 'God is Gracious'.

Well Sean is gracious. He has a gracious approach to things, especially if they are feathered or furry! (Pause.)

He is gracious around the house and if things go wrong or he gets stressed his vocabulary is so gracious, I have to cover my ears!

Well, if I think about that perhaps that job is taken by me – Fred the er ... peaceful ruler.

My mum's name, Clare, has an appropriate meaning 'Clear'. Mum, you are pretty clear about things. You are clear on what you want from life, like being a jewellery maker. You are clear that you are the best mum in the world. When you have to tell me off and send me to bed, well you're pretty clear then too. (Pause.)

The one thing though, on a more serious note, Mum has always been pretty clear on who her perfect man is, that's: incredibly intelligent, talented, witty, charming, amusing and extremely good looking. (Pause.) Naturally this is me, Fred. Sorry Sean, you're a great runner up though.

One last thing before I finish.

Do you know it is tradition that the best man gets the choice of which girl he kisses at a wedding. So (pause) Mum, that's you. (Pause.) Sean, 'Pop', I'd like to welcome you to our family.

Ladies and gentlemen raise your glasses to Clare and Sean, congratulations.

BEST MAN SAMPLE SPEECH 2

Written by the author.

I am very pleased to be giving this speech today and would like to thank Ben (the groom) for his kind words. The bridesmaids and pageboys did a wonderful job I agree. On behalf of them all I would like to thank you for their special gifts.

I was quite surprised when I was asked to be best man for Ben. Why? Well I have been abroad for the past four years and have not really been part of Ben's life recently. I only met his lovely wife Katy a few weeks ago. Naturally, I was thrilled to be best man and it has really brought back many happy moments that Ben and I spent together. Particularly when we were mates at college in Brighton.

At college Ben was always the joker. He kept everyone amused with his jokes and even poked fun at our tutors. He is a great mimic as you all know. I remember one day in particular when our lecturer was late for a class. Ben stood up in front of the room and shook his head to give it a tousled look. He grabbed a pair of glasses from one of the students and then proceeded to mimic our lecturer. He told us a crazy story about a flock of sheep blocking the road and preventing him from arriving at college on time. We all collapsed laughing as he sounded just like our lecturer who lived in the country and was always complaining about the animals on the road. Ben was brilliant and even when the lecturer arrived he carried on. To the lecturer's credit he joined in the laughter too.

Ben is such great company and a fun person to be around. There is however another side to Ben as those close to him will know. He is always there if you are in trouble, and believe me I've had my share of scrapes. He never failed to back me up and has been very supportive along the years. Katy, I am sure you will feel the same and I know he will be a great husband, even if his jokes do drive you mad occasionally.

Let's turn the tables on Ben for a moment shall we? Under four tables I have pasted several pictures of Ben in various guises. Let's take picture one on this table in front of me. Linda can you hold it up please?

(Guests have been asked in advance to hold up the pictures.)

This is a picture of Ben aged three-and-a-half. As you can see he is wearing his mother's blonde wig and his talents as a mimic have begun!

On the next table, Sam, can you take yours out please? This is Ben at 14 dressed in his smart school uniform. However, if you look closely you can see that his cap is back to front, his tie is a black bow tie (not a school tie), his jacket has a pillow down the front and his trousers are rolled up to his knees. This was a character from a comic that was popular at the time and one of Ben's favourites. He looks great doesn't he?

The next picture, Auntie Sue your turn, is of Ben at 18 and this is the depiction of the lecturer I mentioned earlier. This photo was plastered on the front page of the college newspaper and caused much amusement at the time.

Finally, I have the ultimate picture of Ben in the shower taken after his stag night four days ago. With apologies to Katy but I couldn't resist it. He is fully clothed and smiling inanely at the camera. Not as a mimic but just as himself being the crazy but loveable character he is. Your life with Ben will never be dull that's for sure.

Now I have been asked to send you love from Chris and Andrew who are in the USA and couldn't make it today. Also from the folks on the Isle of Wight, Greg and Pam who are looking after the grandchildren and send you 'health, wealth and happiness'.

Katy and Ben we all wish you the very best for the future and 'May the roof above you never fall in, and may you both never fall out!'

Fellow guests please raise your glasses to the happy couple Ben and Katy.

Bride

There may be an opportunity for the bride to give a speech and so here is an example of what she may include:

▶ *Thank special people who have not yet been mentioned or thanked previously.*

- Tell a little story about what attracted you to your husband/partner.
- Mention your parent/s or special relation and find a few kind words to say about them.
- You may also want to mention your grandparents, godparents or step-parent/s.

BRIDE SAMPLE SPEECH

I'd just like to mention what a fantastic day this has been so far. I would like to thank my Aunt Lynn for all her wonderful flower arrangements and my loving sister Martina for her help and support over the past 22 years. But, in particular these last two months!

Ben, I fell for you when I first saw you in a local play – you were acting the part of Puck in A Midsummer Night's Dream and then my dream came true when 18 months later you asked me to be your wife.

Thank you everyone for being here and making this day so very special.

Useful tips

Here is a list of what to do when making a wedding speech:

DO:
- *Prepare well and provide props or visuals.*
- *Think of some amusing stories or events to relate.*
- *Speak slowly and clearly.*
- *Make sure you can be heard (use a microphone if necessary).*
- *Laugh with not at your audience.*
- *Allow time for laughter – pause after a joke.*

When dealing with hecklers – DO:
- *Tell hecklers that this is your turn to speak and theirs will come later.*

- ▶ *Keep off the alcohol before you speak.*
- ▶ *Hold your hand up, ask people to give you the 'air time I deserve' to stop loud or offending remarks.*
- ▶ *Avoid eye contact or arguments with disruptive people.*
- ▶ *Ask to his/her friends 'Is he with you?' when someone is really disruptive (it then becomes their responsibility).*
- ▶ *Smile and carry on regardless.*

If you tend to dry up – DO:
- ▶ *Visualize yourself presenting the speech successfully.*
- ▶ *Practise in front of friends or relations.*
- ▶ *Memorize the first and last line of the speech.*

On the day – DO:
- ▶ *Take a sip of water, breathe and* **carry on.**
- ▶ *Smile, breathe and* **carry on.**
- ▶ *Look at all the friendly faces who want you to do well and* **carry on.**

6

Christenings

In this chapter you will learn:
- *how to use correct etiquette*
- *how to give a short speech for the 'wetting of the baby's head'*
- *how to toast the newly born child.*

So let's start with the baby's name. Usually parents research and ponder over a variety of names before finally making a choice. They look at current trends or consider names from close relations. The names are then selected by parents and registered on the birth certificate.

In England the Church does not believe that the child's ultimate salvation depends on whether a child has been christened or which christening service has been used. The more traditional services are mentioned below but parents are free to choose where and how to name their child. This may be just a simple family gathering at home or a more lavish family celebration.

Usually it is the godparents or chosen guardian of the child who gives a short speech at the reception or family gathering.

Type of service

SERVICES OF BLESSING

These are based on what Jesus did when children were brought to him: 'He took the children in his arms, laid his hands on them, and blessed them' (Mark 10:13–16). The service of *Thanksgiving for the Gift of a Child* in the Church of England's *Common Worship* book (p. 337) is an example.

SERVICES OF DEDICATION

Where the parents make promises about the upbringing of their children. These are often held in Baptist churches.

SERVICES OF INFANT BAPTISM

These declare the child to be a follower of Jesus Christ until such time as he/she can decide what religious path to follow, if at all.

The services mentioned overlap in some cases, and a celebration of the child's birth and life is found in all three.

Becoming a godparent

So you have been asked to be a godparent. What are your duties and why do parents need them? When an infant is baptized he/she can't answer the questions for him/herself, so someone needs to answer them. Godparents (also called sponsors or proxies) were originally introduced into the baptism service for this reason. In the history of the Church godparents also promised to bring the child up in the Christian faith, and took responsibility for this.

At infant baptism, parents may be godparents to their own children. The parents of the child are required to make the selected statements together with the godparents. The role of godparent is, these days, rather like a supportive friend who helps the parents and takes a special interest in the child and their wellbeing.

In the case of a baptism, godparents may be committed Christian believers within the family of the Church. They should be close enough to the family of the child to be able to carry out the responsibilities they have agreed to. They may be baptized and in most cases, confirmed (unless they are members of a church which doesn't have confirmation). However, these are only guidelines and there are no hard and fast rules to adhere to. Many people today are godparents who are not attached to any church but have simply agreed to be the guardian of the child.

Insight

It is usual to take a small gift for the baby – something that lasts is best.

Naturally it is up to your godchild to decide whether or not to follow a religious path when he/she comes of age. There are many different ceremonies according to which religious group you belong to. Some have the equivalent to godparents and some do not. Many people bring their children up with no religious beliefs but follow a spiritual path of their own. The naming of a child does not have to be a religious ceremony but in England this is usually the traditional way.

SPEECH GUIDELINES

- ▶ *Thank the parents for asking you to be a godparent or guardian.*
- ▶ *Mention some aspect of the role that you are looking forward to.*
- ▶ *If requested – name the baby and propose a toast.*

Making a short speech at a christening is not always called for but here are some examples.

GODMOTHER OR GODFATHER SAMPLE SPEECH 1

I am delighted to have been asked as a godmother/father to watch over your newly born son/daughter until he/she becomes of age. This is a wonderful opportunity to support this tiny human being who is a special part of your family. I will make time to show him/her that rainbows are endless and dragons are magic. Today long words are not necessary only joy at this miracle of life.

Then you would name the baby if requested to do so.

GODMOTHER OR GODFATHER SAMPLE SPEECH 2

Thank you for this opportunity to be a godfather/mother to (name of baby). I shall do my best to support him/her throughout his/her life.

_____

Parental thanks

If there is a reception after the christening service this may be the opportunity for the parents to propose a toast to their offspring.

PARENTS' SAMPLE SPEECH

Friends and family I would like to propose a toast to our newly born son/daughter/twins. To (name of baby/ies) may he/she/ they have excellent health, moderate wealth and a great deal of happiness. Cheers.

You could use other words to substitute the usual 'health, wealth and happiness' such as 'a healthy body, an enquiring mind and an adventurous spirit' or 'may he/she have wisdom, self-belief and never lose his/her youthful enquiring mind' or 'I wish him/her butterflies in the sun, stars in the night and wind to blow away all his/her cares.'

7

Milestone birthdays

In this chapter you will learn:
* *how to personalize your message*
* *how to bring in toasts and jokes*
* *how to weave in personal stories and anecdotes.*

Short and punchy

Whole families seldom, if ever, come together as a group, except at weddings, funerals and milestone birthdays. Family celebrations can be fun but they are sensitive occasions. Any member of the family can be chosen to give a speech at a milestone birthday. It is important to choose someone who creates a positive vibe and has some amusing stories or anecdotes to relate. These speeches need to be short and punchy.

When formulating a speech:

▶ *Think about the life of the person you are toasting.*
▶ *What have they achieved and are there any unusual incidents that have occurred?*
▶ *Did they overcome adversity (as in the speech below)?*
▶ *Have they won an award or received a special medal or certificate?*
▶ *Look at their hobbies and interests for inspiration and humour.*

SAMPLE SPEECH FOR A BIRTHDAY

Here is an example of a speech given at a 70th birthday party. The speech was from the author's daughter to her father.

Dad, we are here to celebrate your 70th birthday and I want to tell you about how much you have influenced my life.

I have often been asked where I get my positive attitude from, and I believe it has come mainly from you. I have watched you turn your hand to a number of careers, and you are a true entrepreneur. You have seldom been employed and have gone from being a car salesman to a wine importer and now you run your own estate agency. I have seldom heard you complain and your 'can do' attitude has definitely rubbed off on me.

People often speak about goals and how to achieve them. I often help people to set and achieve goals. So, how have I learnt how to do that?

I remember when you had a particular goal – an unachievable goal it seemed at the time – a goal that the doctors said was impossible.

The injuries you sustained in a car accident several years ago had left your right leg torn in pieces and you had broken your left in three places. I remember visiting you in intensive care. Later when you had recovered a little you told me how you had looked up in disbelief when the doctors said you would NEVER walk again. You were a keen cricketer and had captained the team at Rotingdean CC and you were a well-known umpire at the Sussex County Ground. Never walking again was to you inconceivable. Not only that, I was due to be married eight months later and we both know how you wanted desperately to walk me down the aisle.

I will never forget the day you drew me to your side and whispered in my ear, 'I will walk you down the aisle if it's the last thing I do.'

I cried many tears that night as I knew this would not be possible.

The day of my wedding arrived and I noticed your wheelchair ready by the front door from the upstairs landing. As I came down the stairs in my wedding dress I couldn't believe my eyes. There you were, standing at the bottom of the stairs holding onto the banisters. You had a cane in your other hand and you were beaming all over your face.

You had apparently taken it one step at a time. You told me you had visualized yourself walking me down the aisle on my wedding day, and had seen yourself with strong legs and a proud smile. You had achieved the impossible. Not only were you to play cricket again – which you did the following year. The final amazing achievement was to ski with your grandchildren five years later at the age of 68.

Today I know that my positive attitude is inherited from you. You have given me support and encouragement in everything I have ever attempted.

Thank you for being there for me. Happy 70th Birthday Dad.

'Being 70 years young is sometimes far more cheerful and hopeful than being 40 years old' – O. Holmes.

Here's to my father who is 70 years young and getting younger every day! Cheers.

Jokes, quotes, toasts and anecdotes

Insight
Get ideas from their hobbies, interests and past achievements.

A gathering of family and friends is a good time to bring up special toasts, quotes and jokes if appropriate.

Gloria Hunniford, the well-known radio and TV personality, tells this story to encourage people to adapt jokes and anecdotes to fit the occasion.

A very good friend of mine makes a habit of having a notebook at the ready. He logs every interesting comment, story or joke he hears along the way. He systematically files them under subject headings. This allows him to tailor any of his stories to any kind of subject. It is interesting how a lot of comments that you overhear can be adapted to personal needs. One good example I heard goes as follows:

'Tonight I feel like Elizabeth Tailor's sixth husband. I know exactly what I should be doing, but I'm dammed if I know how to make it different.'

This could be the opener (if you are male) to many a special occasion speech and would raise a laugh right from the start.

If you are female, pick any well-known man who has been married several times:

'Tonight I feel like Charlie Chaplin's third wife...'

Insight
Always adapt your jokes and anecdotes to suit the occasion.

USEFUL QUOTATIONS

Here are some example quotes that can be used for birthdays:

- ▶ *'Real old age begins when one only looks backwards to the past rather than forwards to the future.'*
- ▶ *'Here's to a life well lived – if only I had realized it sooner.'*

- *'If you are told how young you look, then you are obviously getting older.'*
- *'Looking down the ages I feel lucky. I know I can't lose any of them.'*

SOME BIRTHDAY TOASTS AND ANECDOTES

> **Insight**
> Always ask yourself what's important for *them* to hear.

I overheard this toast from a friend whose father had been a captain in the navy.

> *My wife has reached the grand old age of 60. It takes a lot of paint to keep her good looking and look how she's all decked out today. It takes an experienced man to handle her correctly and she can be quite uncontrollable at times. Today she is sailing close to the wind. Showing her topsides, hiding her bottom and when coming in to port she heads for the buoys! To my wife at 60 – cheers.*

This is a great way to personalize a toast. Think about a hobby or interest and weave it in as part of a story.

Here are a few ideas to get you started.

Pottery, fishing, skiing, and salsa dancing
How could you make these personal?

Pottery: She knows how to use her hands. She is creative and likes getting her hands dirty. She is careful and expressive.

> *Here's to my lovely wife on her 30th birthday. She handles her men like she handles her pots, with tender loving care, moulding them to her liking. She's a great cook and her dishes are fired with passion. Doesn't she look dishy tonight!*

Fishing: He sits waiting patiently. He catches the fish and reels it in.

He is a true fisherman. His ideas float slowly to the surface and then he waits patiently while he pulls others round to his way of thinking. Last year he caught the big one and landed the best contract of his career. Now he is celebrating his 40th birthday in style – but is he? No, a little bird told me this is his 50th birthday – he took us all in, hook, line and sinker!

Skiing: She skis downhill and slalom. She is fearless, well balanced and takes the bumps and ruts in her stride.

Today my sister is celebrating her 20th birthday. I have watched her determination to succeed as she sped past the usual ruts along the way. She maintained her balance, kept her poles firmly planted and felt the wind in her hair as she reached her ultimate goal. Here's to my sister – just don't get too pisted! (pardon the pun).

Salsa dancing: She is rhythmic and sways to the sound of the music. She is colourful and enjoys life.

Friends, family and guests, welcome to my mother's 50th birthday. As you all know she teaches salsa dancing. My dad often complains that she dances to a different beat from him and that this often causes discord. However, he has also said that he has learnt to keep to her rhythm for most of the time! I know my mum is a lover of life and my brother and I are more in tune with her now than when we were young, I'm sure. Our lives have been coloured by her bright personality and positive outlook.

So please raise your glasses to our wonderful mum before we dance the night away.

In the examples above you can see how easy it is to personalize your speech. You just need to know a little about the interests and hobbies of the person you are toasting.

8

Funerals

In this chapter you will learn:
- *how to deliver an appropriate message*
- *ideas for the address*
- *appropriate poems and quotes.*

Creating the correct mood and delivering an appropriate message are vital at a funeral. Find out whether the funeral is to be help at a church or a crematorium as the ceremony will differ. As with any special occasion a funeral will be a day to remember special events and moments in a person's life. It is usual for the minister of any religion to say a few words. If the funeral is for one of the regular congregation the minister will also know them well.

Insight
Remember to ask the family what they would like you to say.

Emotions

A little research is necessary and if you have been chosen to speak you will no doubt know the person quite well. It is important to take the feelings of the whole family into consideration. Take time to ask them what they would like you to say and build your speech around that. Add quotes and anecdotes from the life of the deceased to enrich your speech. Remember the acronym KISS – keep it short and simple.

Insight
Keep the speech short, simple and sensitive.

If you feel emotional while speaking fix your mind on something in the room, for example, a person's hat, or focus on a picture or ornament. If you select this beforehand it will help to keep your emotions under control. It is perfectly fine to feel upset or sad but not really helpful if you break down in the middle. However, if this happens don't worry, just dry your eyes and carry on, people will understand. Remember that this is an occasion where you are concentrating on the person who has died. Do not speak about yourself or elaborate too much, as an address should be between three and five minutes at most.

Appropriate words

Insight
Offer comfort and support to the family by mentioning special moments or stories about the person's life.

WELL-KNOWN QUOTES

Quotes are often appropriate at funerals and some are included below. Most will be suitable for any address.

Death is nothing at all. I have only slipped away into the next room. I am I – and you are you. Whatever we were to each other; that we still are. Call me by my old familiar name; speak to me in the easy way which you always used. Put no difference in your tone. Wear no forced air of solemnity or sorrow. Laugh as we always laughed at the little jokes we shared together. Let my name forever be the household word that it always was. Let it

be spoken without effort, without a trace of shadow on it. Life
means all that it ever meant. It is the same as it ever was; there is
unbroken continuity.

Why should I be out of mind because I am out of sight? I am
waiting for you, for an interval, somewhere very near, just around
the corner. All is well.

Henry Scott Holland – Canon of St Paul's Cathedral 1847–1918

A butterfly lights beside us like a sunbeam. And for a brief
moment its glory and beauty belong to our world. But then
it flies on again, and though we wish it could have stayed,
we feel so lucky to have seen it…

Source unknown

Among the flowers blessed by the setting sun
Among the best loved flowers by everyone
There grew a tiny rose that bore no thorn
In every way so perfect, no leaf torn
Who when the rain fell from a sodden sky
To land upon the leaves of those close by
Would turn her pretty head and brightly say
Lift up your heads, it looks like sun today.
One night when all the stars shone in the sky
A misty hand reached out from way up high
And when the sun brought forth another day
That little flower so loved had gone away.

Jackie Arnold – written on the death of my grandmother in 1986

Do not stand on my grave and weep;
I am not there. I do not sleep.
I am a thousand winds that blow.
I am the diamond's glint on snow.
I am the sunlight on ripened grain.
I am the gentle autumn's rain.
When you awaken in the morning's hush,
I am the swift uplifting rush
of quiet birds in circled flight.

I am the soft stars that shine at night.
Do not stand at my grave and cry;
I am not there. I did not die.

Author unknown

PERSONAL RECOLLECTIONS

Personal stories at a funeral are always the best. Tell them with humour and bring out the very best of the person you can. Concentrate on the positive aspects of their life and weave in some magical moments that all will remember. Plan your speech just as you would for any occasion in this book. Bear in mind that you are offering comfort and support to the family at this difficult time.

Insight

Keep the speech focused on the happy events and achievements of the deceased.

SAMPLE SPEECH OF A LIFE LIVED AND LOST

On this day we are here to celebrate the life of my wonderful friend [name]. You will all know that we first met while we were both at primary school and our friendship has been long and very rewarding. Why do I say that? Well, to begin with she had an amazing sense of humour. If I was feeling low she would always have an encouraging word to say, I always felt her support during both the good times and the bad. She was the kind of person who would always give time to those close to her and would think of others' needs before her own.

She was quite ill one year after a bout of flu that affected many of us. For many years she had made hot meals for several of the pensioners in the village and during that period she never missed a day, even when she should have been in bed recovering.

I remember she joked about her advancing age and said, 'I feel just like that old oak tree in the corner of the field, past my prime but refusing to budge!'

To conclude I will leave you with the amusing words of Sir Winston Churchill, someone she greatly admired, 'I am ready to meet my maker, whether my maker is ready for the ordeal of meeting me, is another matter.'

We know that unlike Sir Winston [name] will be welcomed by her maker with open arms.

I know that you will all join me in offering our deepest sympathy to all her family and friends. She will be missed but her spirit will live on in our memories.

10 THINGS TO REMEMBER

1 *Remember the three Ps: Plan, Prepare and Practise. Practise to the point where you do not need notes.*

2 *Make sure your speech is appropriate to the occasion. Weddings vary, as do all other significant family occasions, and so should your research.*

3 *Always ensure that you have names and anecdotes correct.*

4 *Focus on the audience and not on yourself.*

5 *If gifts are required, think about how you will deliver these.*

6 *At weddings, start strongly and end on a positive note. Consider including some props or visuals.*

7 *Channel your nerves. Breathe, smile and have fun.*

8 *At christenings, keep the speech short and light-hearted.*

9 *If you are a godparent, mention what you are looking forward to in your role.*

10 *At funerals, remember the good times. If you feel emotion, pause and allow yourself to recover.*

Part three
Speaking at other events

9

After dinner events

In this chapter you will learn:
* *how to collect ideas*
* *how to open with a bang*
* *how to be comfy with comedy*
* *how to deal with hecklers.*

If you are asked to give an after dinner speech you will generally have a few weeks' notice. These are the questions you need to ask yourself:

▶ *Who is my audience and what would they like to hear?*
▶ *What is the make-up of the audience and what are their ages?*
▶ *Have they attended this event before?*
▶ *Who has spoken at this event in the past and what were the topics?*
▶ *Is there a speaker before or after me?*
▶ *What will they be speaking about?*
▶ *What are the formalities and correct etiquette?*
▶ *Will I need to introduce another speaker?*

Then as you begin to formulate your ideas ask:

▶ *What topics would suit this audience?*

Etiquette

At a formal dinner you, as the speaker, may be asked to say grace before people begin to dine. If you are introduced by the chairperson, they will normally ask for silence before asking you to proceed. You then ask that everyone rise before beginning to speak. You may be asked to select your own grace and the most common is:

For what we are about to receive, may the Lord make us truly thankful.

After the meal another tradition you may like to consider is the Loyal Toast. This is always the first toast of the meal and is often delivered during coffee. This toast is recognized in Britain and in all commonwealth countries that recognize the Queen as head of state. If the audience is multicultural it is usual to include other toasts to their heads of state as a courtesy. The toast to the Queen would go as follows:

Ladies and Gentlemen, please be upstanding for the loyal toast – Her Majesty The Queen.

Proposing the toast

If you are proposing a lengthy toast to an organization, club or association, the format is as follows:

▶ *A series of sincere compliments or achievements.*
▶ *Then a short amusing anecdote or relevant joke.*
▶ *Finally the toast itself.*

For example, if you are toasting the achievements of the local speakers' club you might say:

> *Fellow members, the club has exceeded all our expectations this year. The efforts of [name the President and the committee] have been outstanding. The overall membership has risen, the standard of the speeches has improved and we have won the regional competition twice. This is an amazing achievement and has been largely due to the dedication of the committee and the enthusiasm of the members. As you know we hosted this year's International Competition and the atmosphere was electric as one of our members managed to come second. We were all very proud of this excellent placing and wish her well in the next heat. (Series of compliments.)*
>
> *Here are some little quotes to help her on her way to speaking success:*
>
> *'Stage fright? It's not the stage that frightens me – it's the audience! Now I always check on them before they check on me!'*
>
> *'Visualize your audience standing up as one and applauding your success – it's very motivating!'*
>
> *'Remember that 80 per cent of how well the speech is received is determined before you step onto the stage.'*
>
> *Finally,*
>
> *'When you ski down a mountain you feel the rush of adrenalin and you react quickly when someone blocks your path. You get*

up after a fall and you know you'll learn by your mistakes. You feel that buzz when your technique is working and you are able to relax and enjoy yourself. So when you speak in public be like that skier, enjoy the moment and then afterwards make sure you take advantage of the 'Après speech'.'

(Then perhaps a quote and/or joke. And finally the toast to conclude the proceedings.)

Mr President and fellow club members, we thank you all for your contributions to this year's success and here's to many more of the same. Please raise your glasses and toast the [name] Speakers' Club.

Insight
Look at what they have heard before, to avoid repetition.

REPLYING TO THE TOAST

If you are considering a reply to the toast then a little preparation is needed. Obviously you will not know exactly what will be said, but as it is usual to compliment the club, organization or association you can prepare a short reply.

- ▶ *Thank the speaker for the kind words.*
- ▶ *Refer back to one of the more memorable comments.*
- ▶ *Give further information about your achievements.*
- ▶ *Repeat your thanks.*

For example:

On behalf of the speakers' club I would like to thank you very much for your kind words. (Thanks)

We were particularly pleased when new members started to sign up and this has given us a new lease of life. It has been fascinating to watch the newer speakers progress through their manuals and achieve their awards.

(Reference to one of the comments.)

Last year we had six members who achieved their CTM, two their CTM bronze and three their Competent Leader Awards. We added four ribbons to our club banner and ended the year with over 30 members.

(Further information.)

So on behalf of all the club members and the committee we thank you for your toast. (Thanks)

Your message and theme

So, how do you get ideas for after dinner speeches? Well, speech ideas are everywhere. They can come from events in the newspapers, from incidents in daily life, from topics discussed on the radio or TV, or just pop into your head in the shower. Begin collecting ideas and store them in whichever way is convenient for you. Cards in a shoebox, Post-its on the wall, lists on the computer, you decide. Remember, ideas which grab your enthusiasm are those you are more likely to deliver with vitality. Think about your audience and what they want to hear. What would interest or amuse them?

What is your goal for this topic? Is there a message you want your audience to take home with them? Do you just want to entertain? Is the speech a call to action?

Develop a theme and then insert a catchphrase that will encapsulate your ideas. If, for example, the theme is 'Life and our choices', you could insert this observation by Albert Einstein both at the beginning and end of your speech:

> *There are only two ways to live your life, one is as though nothing were a miracle, the other is as though everything were a miracle.*

The main body of the speech could then include stories about both attitudes.

Start with a bang

Use a quote or saying that you heard/found and is relevant to your speech topic. Internet research will help you to find a wealth of quotes and really create interest from the start.

Speech openers are what you win or lose your audience with. The first impression is so vital it is worth taking the time to do a little research. In Chapter 1 we looked at metaphors as a way of introducing humour. They are also very good openers; they are unexpected and give a twist that gains attention.

USE METAPHORS

This is using something that is equal to something else and conjures up a visual in the listener's mind. It visually pierces through barriers to understanding. For example 'the internet is a superhighway' is a metaphor because the internet acts like a motorway and transports information. Other examples include: 'She's an accident waiting to happen', 'Oh my computer's crashed!', 'All the world's a stage...', 'Time waits for no one', 'The sales have just crash landed, what will it take to get them flying again?'

Ask yourself what do I know about this audience from which I can draw a metaphor? Are they interested in sport, travel, current events, business or entertainment? All these are rich sources of metaphor. Be very aware of cultural, generational and value differences and be selective when choosing.

> **Top tip**
> Remember, KISSER – keep it short, simple, effective and relevant.

Other ways of opening your speech are by using:

- ▶ *a startling fact or statistic*
- ▶ *a short story*
- ▶ *a challenging question.*

Comedy and humour

Laughing with others is a sure way to endear yourself to the audience. Getting people smiling and feeling good about the event creates immediate rapport. It shows you care and want to evoke empathy. It builds confidence in both you as a speaker and those in the audience. Laughter is very inclusive and brings people closer, which in turn leads to positive repartee. It is wonderful as an ice-breaker.

Insight

Don't be afraid to insert a little humour, or tell a story or two.

The opposite is true of negative or cutting humour, which is to be avoided at all costs. An African quote keeps this in perspective and is a useful reminder that this kind of humour can be hurtful and inappropriate, 'You don't have to blow out my candle to make yours grow brighter.'

Use humour to allow others to laugh at you or with you. Humour should not be at the expense of someone else. Laughing with others leaves people with whole self-esteem and is nourishing. Look for ways to maximize the positive and minimize the negative aspects of humour.

RECORDING AND REHEARSING

Heard a good joke recently? Have you forgotten the punchline? Yes, this is quite common but it is also avoidable. If you know you have to make a speech listen out for a good joke and – this is key – write it down. If you don't have time to write it down, pick up your mobile phone and send it to your voicemail! Then tell someone the joke as soon as you can so that it stays with you. Visualize the joke in your mind. Give characters a face and put the joke in familiar surroundings. Keep a file on your computer with a variety of jokes and humorous incidents to spice up your speeches. Give the files subject headings for particular events. Do the same with amusing stories, quotes and anecdotes.

There are not many people who can tell a joke or anecdote without rehearsing it well. It is a myth that great speakers are spontaneous. On the contrary, they have practised so long that it *looks* spontaneous. Try following these easy steps to really perfect your joke telling:

1 *Select a joke or anecdote you would like to tell and visualize it (avoid sex, religion and politics).*
2 *Repeat the joke three times in front of a mirror using appropriate facial expressions.*
3 *Practise pausing for the count of five before saying the punchline.*
4 *If you can, record the joke/anecdote onto a tape and play it back to yourself to hear what it sounds like.*
5 *Ask a friend or family member to give you honest feedback.*
6 *Practise until you have it word perfect.*

Top tips

▶ *Be sensitive to your audience and avoid subjects that will offend.*
▶ *Trying to mimic an accent or a funny voice is disastrous unless you do it perfectly.*
▶ *Speak at a measured pace as a joke needs excellent timing – don't rush it.*
▶ *Make eye contact with your audience. Involve them if you can.*
▶ *Listen to the responses and react to them.*
▶ *Give your audience time to laugh.*
▶ *Speed up if you feel a lull in the energy.*
▶ *Refrain from laughing at your own joke or amusing story.*
▶ *Believe in your ability to deliver confidently.*
▶ *Keep it brief and leave the audience wanting more.*

SAMPLE AFTER DINNER SPEECH 1

Below is a humorous example of an after dinner speech. There are comments in brackets to help you with pauses and ideas for making the speech your own. The speech is divided into the introduction, three main sections forming the body of the text and the conclusion. It is vitally important to find out in advance how much time is allowed for your speech. The speech below would generally take between eight and ten minutes. When giving a speech the words are delivered at a slower pace (85–110 words per minute) than when you are reading (320–360 words per minute). In a speech there are pauses, time for expressions and gestures, plus allowances for laughter. Make sure your timing is accurate. Be prepared to change the timing if your event is running late. There is nothing worse than a speaker overrunning his/her allotted time slot, as no doubt you agree.

Doing the Right Thing

By Steve Roberts

▶ Introduction

For My Queen and Country. What would you do for our Queen and Country?

Most welcome guests, this is what I did for my Queen and Country...

A few years ago I was lucky enough to go to China on a very important business trip with two work colleagues Peter and Ken. Our boss told us we had to be on our best behaviour and act as ambassadors for our Queen and Country.

We had an excellent flight to Beijing. The food was delicious, the entertainment was great – just a shame our bags ended up in Hong Kong. (Pause for laughter.) On arriving in Beijing we were met by our hosts who had arranged a banquet in our honour that evening. I could feel panic gushing through my whole body. We had *(pause for effect)* no clothes. Fortunately, Ken and I managed to buy ourselves some suits, but Peter was having problems.

(Little aside to the audience, drawing them into the story.) Mind you with a 23 inch neck, 56 inch chest and a sumo wrestler's waistline, he was always going to have problems!

We finally fitted him out in a lovely pair of black trousers and a black turtleneck jumper which somehow made him look taller. I put this down to his sleeves; if they were five inches longer they would at a push, have reached his wrists.

▶ Chicken's foot *(bullet point reminder for next section)*

We arrived at the Banquet and apologized for Peter, *(raised eyebrows and aside to the audience)* now looking like a self-conscious Mafia hit man who had lost the will to live. *(Pause.)*

There must have been about a dozen of us seated around a large circular table and at the beginning of the meal our host gave us a toast 'Gambei'. This was the first of many.

Our first dish looked vaguely like soup. I put my spoon in and hit something solid and when I pulled it out I thought to myself 'Oh my god what's that?' On closer inspection I could see it was a chicken's foot. I didn't know what to do with it, *(looking around at your audience)* what do you do with it?

Do you nibble it, *(mime this)* do you crunch it *(mime this)* or do you put it on a key ring for luck *(pause so the audience can think about this)*. I had no idea. I quickly glanced around to see if anyone was looking at me. *(Look behind you.)* When the coast was clear, I quickly picked up the chicken foot and dropped it into the serviette on my lap and placed it into my trouser pocket. *(Carry out all these actions with or without a serviette.)* *(Pause.)*

Then, for my Queen and Country, I quickly slurped down a spoonful of soup which tasted similar to the mouthwash at my dentist, regrettably the only difference being I couldn't spit it out. (Stand looking disgusted.) (Longer pause.)

▶ Sea slug

After a few more dishes, the like of which I had never tasted before and for that matter never want to taste again, everyone was given a bowl with a lid. I gingerly removed the lid and was suddenly struck by a most awful stench (turn your head away) which attempted to penetrate my body by wafting up my nose. Fearing asphyxiation, I quickly put my hand over my nose and mouth, pretending I had a cough. (Pause and cough.)

Once I was able to breathe again, my attention was drawn to the contents of the bowl. Mineral, vegetable or animal (say these slowly with a question in your voice) – I'm still not sure. Peter told me it was sea slugs (pause) and promptly put one in his mouth. As he sank his teeth in – (pause) it exploded. As Peter started choking violently I quickly jumped up with my glass and in order to divert attention away from Peter, I toasted our hosts 'Gambei'. Fortunately, Peter quickly recovered.

Not wanting to offend our host and for my Queen and Country I placed a fat, slimy, juicy sea slug into my mouth – I had already decided that I was going swallow it down in one. I took a deep gulp and it slowly slithered down towards my stomach. (Long pause while you look very uncomfortable.) But suddenly a little voice in my head called out 'Hey, there's no way you're keeping that down' and suddenly I could feel it galloping back up (look down at your stomach in alarm). I quickly grabbed my handkerchief, pretending to blow my nose and with slight of hand I transferred the slug into the handkerchief and placed it in my trouser pocket – where it could have nibbled on the chicken foot – but naturally, (pause) it was a vegetarian.

▶ Rice

After about 20 different courses I still hadn't eaten anything tasty when my attention was attracted to a great big bowl of rice coming out, I thought 'thank you Lord something I can finally eat.' And, as it was put on the table and swung slowly round to me, everyone was ignoring it. I thought 'no, not me I'm going to dive into the rice.' As I was about to dive in, a hand gently rested on my shoulder. I turned around and the interpreter said, 'Don't eat the rice'. I said, 'Don't eat the rice?' He replied, 'it would be a sign of disrespect, because it means you haven't had enough food.'

(You sigh.) So, once again (pause) for my Queen and Country, I let the rice go and also any chance of satisfying my appetite.

▶ Conclusion

In conclusion, our hosts were very hospitable and went to great lengths to ensure that we had a meal to remember. (Pause with your eyebrows raised.) May I say they definitely succeeded.

As we were about to leave I asked our host, 'Do you really enjoy eating chicken feet and slugs?' He said, 'I don't know, we only give them to visitors.'

Fellow guests, ladies and gentlemen, let us raise our glasses and extend a toast to our wonderful dinner this evening – cheers!

This is a great example of how to change an amusing incident into a humorous speech. You could base your ideas around any time you had been out to a foreign restaurant. Your unusual or disastrous holiday experience could be turned into a speech, as could your cultural blunders when abroad. Give it a try.

SAMPLE AFTER DINNER SPEECH 2

The second example of a suitable after dinner speech is on the general theme of 'Integrity'. This is a speech that has the intention of making a point or giving the audience something to think/talk about. Once again, pauses and comments are given in brackets. For your own information the speech is again divided into introduction, main text and conclusion, but you would not say this when giving your speech.

Note: This speech would also be suitable for a sales presentation or at a business event.

Integrity – The ransom of modern society

By Adam Broomfield-Strawn

Fellow guests

▶ Introduction

The Roget's Thesaurus definition of integrity is honour.

Some of its synonyms for integrity include: honesty, purity, righteousness, sincerity and virtue.

Samuel Johnson, the eighteenth-century author wrote of integrity: 'There can be no friendship without confidence and no confidence without integrity.'

Integrity is one of the most highly valued qualities sought after in candidates applying for upper management and leadership positions.

So what does Laslo Nagy, the secretary-general for the world organization of the scout movement, mean when he says the following: 'The central need of our times is to find the road we lost or abandoned, and to recover the values we have rejected in favour of every man for himself in pursuit of egoistic goals.'?

Allow me to demonstrate what I believe Laslo means with a little audience participation.

Please raise your right hand like so (raising right hand) if you believe that you live your life with integrity. Your social life, family life and your work life. (Pause.)

(All hands go up.)

Now, keeping your right hand raised, also raise your left hand if you believe that at some time, whether intentionally or unintentionally, you have acted <u>without</u> integrity. I know I have. (And again, all hands go up.)

Thank you for your honesty.

(Pointing both hands at the audience like guns.)

Keep your hands in the air. (Pause.) Ladies and gentlemen, this is a stick-up. (Pause.) Please allow me to introduce myself; my name is 'SOCIETY'. Now, as quickly and quietly as possible I'd like you to hand over your valuables and I will place them in the bag marked 'RESULTS'. (You do not need a bag but turn your palms upwards and motion them towards you as if you are taking something from them.)

Thank you so much for your cooperation, you may now put your hands down.

'But', I hear you say, 'you haven't taken anything'. (Pause.)

Oh, but I have. (Pause and step/lean a little towards the audience.)

The valuables I have taken are your ethics, your morals, your principles and your integrity. (Say these words slowly and with emphasis.)

This is the position we are forced to adopt (put both your hands in the air again) by a society that says – 'Results rule.'

By a society that promotes – 'Winning at all costs.'

And by a society that believes – 'Material wealth is everything and spiritual wealth means nothing.'

Everywhere we look, we see rules being bent or broken, corners being cut and shortcuts being taken (with emphasis). The easy route over the straight and narrow.

From the janitor mopping around the bins but not under them, to the teacher helping a pupil pass another exam to hit another government target. From the athlete taking a banned substance to ensure victory to the businessman fixing prices to retain share value and keep his job.

Yet we still tell our children that cheats never prosper and crime doesn't pay.

They say the cosmetics industry has more than doubled in the last ten years. With society having two faces – are we surprised?

(Note: The above examples can be changed to match your particular occasion/group.)

Trust, confidence and credibility are the victims of today's society in our quest for success – at any cost.

▶ Conclusion

Therefore, fellow guests, I decided a long time ago that I would NOT compromise MY integrity for the sake of results, regardless of financial reward or the status to be gained. I would not mack, hustle, scam or con. If it could not be done clean, it would not be done.

Was it an easy decision to make? (Pause and look around.) Absolutely.

Has it been an easy decision to uphold? (Pause and look around.) Absolutely not.

Now, I do not believe that you <u>have</u> to raise your hand and pledge 'Integrity, always'.

But I <u>do</u> believe that you <u>do not</u> have to raise both hands and be held to ransom.

Handling the hecklers

Hecklers generally fall into three categories:

1 *The after-a-good-meal 'drunk'.*
2 *The 'know it all'.*
3 *The 'confrontational'.*

If you are speaking to guests who have had a lot to drink the chances are you will be heckled at some point. There is no point in trying to out-do drunks or 'know-it-all' types. The best way to deal with them is to make a joke: 'Hey, this is my bit, give me a break' or 'Hey, your part in this comes later, I've got the floor for now' or 'Great comments, time to move on.' You can also involve his/her colleagues by saying, 'Hey, is this man/woman with you?', which will shame them into trying to quieten their colleague down.

If things get really out of hand, have someone you previously briefed give an urgent message to the offending guest so they can be removed (a good idea if you know the drinks are flowing).

Sometimes people may disagree with your views and voice their opinion loudly. Once again, make light of the situation. Do not use comments that will provoke them into further discussion. The best solution is to say, 'We obviously see things differently – that's OK with me and I hope with you too.' Then move swiftly on. Always be respectful and polite no matter what. After all, this is not about how you appear to the audience it's about how you handle yourself.

If you have someone who is 'an expert', allow them to give their views and then gently say, 'I'd like to move on now but I am grateful for your comments.' Or, if they are being really intrusive, 'If we have time at the end of this session, I'd like to include your thoughts. Right now I need to move on.' Smile and do just that, avoiding eye contact if at all possible.

If you are in a group and this person is always jumping in with comments, just hold your hand up and face someone else with the words 'Thanks for your useful comments X, I'd just like to see if others have comments at this point.'

Top tip

Once again, always be polite and respectful. Speak calmly, breathe slowly and stay in control.

10

Sports events

In this chapter you will learn:
- *how to identify your purpose*
- *how to inject a touch of humour*
- *how to prepare a vote of thanks.*

Three key principles

So, you've been asked to give a speech at your local sports club. Is there a purpose? Are you giving out awards, raising funds, thanking the members? Whatever your purpose, there are three things to keep in mind:

1 *The theme.*
2 *The impact.*
3 *The memory.*

Start by deciding on your theme for the event. What is your mission? What will they be expecting? How can you leave them with a good memory of the event?

Always ask WIIFT – What's In It For Them?

Once you have a theme, develop your ideas by writing down short notes as they occur to you.

When considering structure the rule of three also applies here:

1 *How will you open – quote, anecdote, story?*
2 *What is the main body of text? Structure your points into a logical order.*
3 *How will you conclude – toast, joke, vote of thanks?*

Do some research, as it is vital you do not leave anyone out. Be sure to get all the names correct on the night. Ask who has contributed to the success of the club and who needs a special mention.

Insight
Remember, always ask WIIFT – What's In It For Them?

Getting down the bare bones

The following is an example of how to draft your speech ideas before you actually write or record the finished version. This is an amusing speech about toilets in ski resorts presented to the members of a ski club in Kent. The first ideas are listed below:

- *the gear/the outfits*
- *the first incident*
- *don't want to cause a stink/lift the lid on the alpine loos*
- *up at the top, ski down, need toilets*
- *always at the bottom of red or black run*
- *Italians – masters of style and Ferrari etc.*
- *five flights of stairs in ski boots*
- *toilets under water – no lock on the door*
- *industrial toilet paper*
- *you have to pay for them*
- *timer switch – lights go out and doors open*
- *up in the mountains – window exposes you*
- *flat in France – own toilets – wonderful views*
- *that's why we do it!*

Once the ideas are down they are ordered into a beginning, middle and conclusion.

Remember to ask yourself:

- ▶ *What would be best to open with?*
- ▶ *How will the points flow best?*
- ▶ *What would make a good ending?*
- ▶ *What would particularly appeal to my audience?*
- ▶ *How can I engage them in the stories?*
- ▶ *What research will I need to do beforehand?*
- ▶ *Are there any amusing incidents that I need to add?*
- ▶ *Do I need to include a special toast after my speech?*
- ▶ *Who needs a special mention?*
- ▶ *Who do I need to thank?*

Insight

Engage your audience by making the speech relevant to them with stories and anecdotes they can relate to.

SAMPLE SPEECH FOR A SPORTS EVENT

Here is an example of the first part of the speech from the ideas above:

▶ Opening

Fellow members. Is it really worth the hassle? Do I really want to put myself through this torture every year?

(Strong opening, gets them thinking and is amusing.)

The gear is bad enough – less than flattering hat, goggles that make you look like biggles, moon eyes where the sun was blocked, sun tan lotion making you sticky and greasy, need I go on? (Props used here would add to the fun and help to create atmosphere.)

Then there are those boots; hard, inflexible, impossible to get off and walking to the nearest ski lift is a major achievement. Do we really <u>enjoy</u> this?

(Asking a question gets the audience involved.)

Then there is the outfit. I didn't realize I looked like a moon walker until one day I caught a glimpse of myself in the mirror. Let's face it, it's not the most elegant of attire. First, there's the thermals, the long-johns and the roll-neck plus the more modern 'buff' to keep your neck warm. There are the thick wool socks and the coloured hats all to be put on in the centrally heated apartment. Oh and don't forget the sunblock, lip salve, sunglasses, goggles, your ski pass, your ski sticks and down in the basement – three floors down – your skis! By the time we are out of the door I feel like having a shower. And I'm supposed to be on holiday.

▶ First incident

So, there we are, all prepared and ready to queue for the ski lift. Up comes a small boy who is part of the ski school for the under tens. Little 'Pierre' pushes in and promptly stands on your skis so you can no longer move. You have your thick padded gloves on, which makes showing your ticket a major task and then there you are standing on the coloured line waiting for the chair lift to appear. 'Wham' it slams into the back of your knees sending you and your skis backwards with an undignified smack onto the seat. Of course, little Pierre has managed to get onto the same seat and has his ski pole dangerously near your left eye.

(These stories are taken from the experience of the speaker. However, anyone in the audience will identify with these experiences, as they are all members of a ski club.)

Top tip

Plan each part of the speech and write it out in the order you have chosen as in the speech above. Put in your pauses and notes as you go. Decide on your ending and then go back to your questions to see if you have answered them all.

Spicing it up

Speeches at sports events lend themselves to a bit of humour. Jokes go down well after a few drinks. People like to be entertained and will go away with pleasant memories.

How could you make your speech remarkable? Are there any startling facts or situations you could weave in? How can you twist an amusing incident so that you amaze your audience? Can you share an anecdote? Personal stories always make an impact. No two people have the same story to tell and your unique take on it will always have a different perspective.

Tailor your humour to your audience. Introduce jokes that they can relate to. It's also vital for you to be relaxed so don't do slapstick if you are usually a quiet person. Make sure it fits with your own personality so it comes across as believable. Get some funny relevant quotes to drop in and don't over do it.

Remember that humour needs perfect timing. The only way to really hone your skills is to practise. Put in the pauses after the jokes to allow time for laughter. Make sure you pause a little before the punchline to create suspense. Once you have all the parts of your speech prepared try it out on friends and family. Planning, preparation and practise are key. Your speech will then be memorable and have a lasting impact.

Sports stories of overcoming hardship and getting to the top can be very motivating. Look for top sports personalities and tell their story. Then relate it to your club or organization. Use the stories of winning and teamwork to motivate your members.

Insight
Motivate your audience by relating stories of overcoming hardship or adversity.

► Conclusions and vote of thanks

Following on from the first part of the speech above you can then conclude:

So off we go every ski season and some of us more than once.

For what? Well, how does it feel to stand at the summit of a mountain and look across at stunning scenery surrounding you? How great does it feel when you have just skied down a wonderful run with the wind in your hair and at one with nature?

Plus, we can all celebrate today and toast the success of the club's teams in this year's super G for the over fifties, and with a win in the downhill from the juniors. Well done to you all. I would like to thank all those who gave up their time to train our teams and a special thanks goes to... (various people are named as having supported the club) and here's to next year – please raise your glasses to our great club and its members. Cheers.

Insight

Humour and stories need practice, so taking time for this will pay off in the long run.

Accepting awards

SAMPLE SPEECH FOR A SPORTS CLUB TROPHY

Manchester United we were NOT

By David Robertson

► Introduction

As manager of Forest Row Juniors, I cannot not be compared to Sir Alex Ferguson because, whilst pressure is still felt, the level of enjoyment is infinitely better. This team is not really expected to win but I am there to teach the boys to have fun and get some fresh air in their lungs. I was invited to manage the boys aged between 13 and 15 years three years ago. When I became manager it was the boys first time playing a complete 11-a-side on a full-size pitch, with a big goal, so surely they would score more goals than on a six-a-side pitch – that year not so.

▶ Main text

The principle at Forest Row is that the manager stays with the same group of players during their development, so I get to know the individual boys.

Because I am not under any pressure to win every game the committee and myself want every squad member (16 players in all) to have an equal chance to play.

Our league position, as you all know, has been second to bottom, bottom and bottom of division three. An example of our first season record was as follows:

Played – 20

Won – 3

Drew – 0

Lost – 17

Goals scored 17 against 132

Tonight it is my pleasure to introduce you to some of the team and share with you some of the challenges we faced this year.

Let's take Igor and Thomas – both lads are Russian and firm friends. They do not mind where they play as long as they play. However, their parents are members of the nearby Church of Scientology, and no physical contact is permitted, a slight problem, as despite their enjoyment (pause) last year we conceded 132 goals. This year well...

Then there's Adam. Now Adam is a small lad with incredible ball control, his ball control is his strength, but his ability to pass the ball has been a major weakness. Often he finds himself surrounded by five of the opposition with the ball at his feet and nowhere to run. Of course, we also had no goalkeeper this season – now this presents a major problem, as the rules state quite clearly, 'must have a goalkeeper'. So, this season all the boys took a turn. Eventually we got a goalkeeper, but that's another story.

Now John's parents arrived at a training session midway through the season and asked if their son could join the football team. Strangely I noticed that during the conversation John sat in his parents' car.

Well of course I said, he would be welcomed, however, when he got out of the car I could see that he had a clubfoot. His father hastily explained that John really wanted to play football and his parents would understand that John's games would probably be limited. However, tonight I am going to tell you about John's first goal.

Picture the scene – his position is left wing, he has instructions to chase after long balls. On this occasion a long ball is kicked over the opposition's defence and John begins to run. He is now well clear of the other team, so he kicks the ball on, the opposite goalkeeper approaches. I am running down the touchline and as the defender got closer to John I shout, 'kick the ball, John, just kick the ball towards the goal.'

John kicks and the ball sails high, well over the goalkeeper and appears to be heading over the bar. So, John just turns looking rather forlorn and says, 'Sorry David.' (Pause.)

But as I watch, the ball loses impetus and dips about half an inch below the bar.

I turn to John, who has his back to the goal, 'No need to apologize you've just scored a great goal!' John turned, and beamed with delight. Later, when his father collected him he retold the story with genuine pride.

Alex – now where can I start on the tale of Alex? I will always remember one occasion. I used to play Alex as a centre forward, as he was very strong and because of his height the opposition were a little reluctant to tackle him. One day because I wanted to stop goals being conceded I played Alex in defence, but I agreed to let him take any penalties and go up front for corners.

During the match Alex got the ball in his own penalty area and as the opposition backed away Alex continued to run with the ball. All his teammates were screaming for the ball but still Alex ran on, and on, and on until he reached the opposition penalty area. He steadied himself and a goal looked certain. But no, a lad from the opposition managed to get the ball and clear the danger – so he thought.

Alex turned and chased him halfway down the pitch, and eventually recovered the ball. He made a great effort, passed it to his teammate and together they created a wonderful winning goal.

So, we have finished the season on a high despite our difficulties and I would like to congratulate all the team for their efforts this year. As I mentioned we had a pretty poor record and the team has faced many challenges. However, I am proud to announce that this year we have:

Played – 22

Won – 12

Drawn – 6

Lost only – 4

Goals scored 123 against 98

On behalf of the team I would like to ask Alex to come up and accept the cup and once again well done to everyone on your fantastic achievement.

When accepting awards as a captain or team member it is usual to make a very short speech to thank other members of the team.

This year was a challenge for us but we would like to thank David for his support and encouragement. We are delighted to receive this cup and each of us will keep it for a few weeks in our bedrooms – I have bagged the first turn, sorry lads! Thanks to everyone and I'm told there's some good food to be had in the hall. Let's go!

11

Retirement

In this chapter you will learn:
- *about collecting the facts*
- *how to strike the right note*
- *how to give an appropriate send off.*

> *The closing years of life are like the end of a masquerade party – when the masks are dropped.*
>
> Schopenhauer

Key ingredients

If you have been requested to give a speech at a retirement party it will be useful to do your homework. Your speech will probably contain the following elements:

▶ *the reason for the retirement*
▶ *a few interesting facts about the person's life*
▶ *some achievements*
▶ *sincere comments and memories*
▶ *a drop of humour*
▶ *a mention of the future*
▶ *a toast.*

Before giving your speech talk to members of the recipient's close family or friends. Ask about amusing incidents, past achievements, quirky habits and if the recipient has any interesting hobbies. Also try to find out what plans they have for retirement as this will add useful information when buying a gift and planning your toast. The same will be needed in a business context but here you will need to consult colleagues as well as family and friends.

If they are leaving due to ill health or have been forced to retire you will need to consider these thoughts and feelings sensitively. Be sincere, and end on a positive note for the future. This is where a good quote can be very useful.

Insight
Speak to family and friends to find out key facts and stories.

USING A QUOTE TO PROVIDE THE RIGHT WORDS

▶ *'Now you can give up being what everyone else wants you to be – you can be yourself. Now you are retiring you will have the time.'*
▶ *'To be surprised in life is surely one of the best ways to stay young.'*
▶ *Cicero once said 'I am profoundly grateful to old age, which has increased my eagerness for conversation and taken away that for food and drink.'*
▶ *'In retirement you get the chance to do all those things you talked about doing but put off.'*

Insight
Quotes, proverbs and short poems give life to any speech.

Giving a good send off

It is important to give a good send off to anyone retiring. They may be feeling a bit redundant and find it hard to come to terms with their increased leisure time. You have spoken about their achievements and added a couple of amusing quotes or anecdotes. Now for the lasting memory and parting gift. You will have done a little research into what would be appropriate in the circumstances. Here are some examples of a good send off.

> **Insight**
>
> You need to know what plans they have for retirement and weave this into your speech.

Someone retiring naturally at the end of a good career:

> *On behalf of XYZ Company we would like to congratulate you on your retirement and wish you all the very best of luck for the future. We would like you to accept this gift as a token of our appreciation.*
>
> *We hope that your retirement will be as successful as your career with us and wish you well for the future. We take pleasure in offering you this farewell gift on behalf of us all.*

For someone leaving due to ill health and this is known to all:

> *We know that X is leaving us earlier than planned and we all wish him/her a speedy recovery (or health and happiness for the future). On behalf of us all we would like to present you with this small gift of...*

For someone who is leaving due to ill health and it is unknown to staff:

> *Everyone here wishes you a relaxing time ahead. We hope that you will not forget your colleagues at X company (you can add a personal reason here). Please accept this gift as a token of our thanks.*

> **Insight**
>
> End with a lasting memory and a parting gift.

Top tip

Most important is to leave the person with a feeling of contentment despite the reasons for leaving. If you can strike a balance, and bring in some amusement and speak with sincerity, your speech will be successful.

12

Prize/award ceremonies

In this chapter you will learn:
- *how to carry out important research*
- *how to make the award ceremony memorable*
- *how to accept an award gracefully.*

Presenting an award

Presenting an award in the right way can be as important as the award itself.

The positive impact and lasting impression of receiving an award can be totally lost if: the award is not signed and the winner needs to ask for a signature; if the award is handed over without a smile or word of encouragement; if it is handed over upside down; or if the name on the award is misspelt.

Insight

Always hand over an award or certificate with a smile and words of encouragement.

Make sure you make time for a little advanced research. Ask yourself what you can do to make the award ceremony memorable. Here are some questions to consider:

- *What is the name of the recipient? How can you ensure the spelling is correct?*
- *What is the award for and is there a tradition associated with it?*
- *What do you know about the recipient that would interest the audience?*
- *Why was this person chosen to receive the award?*
- *What would this person like you to say (ask the friends and relations)?*
- *Where will you stand to present the award?*
- *If the award is on a table where would it be best to place it (avoid turning your back to the audience if at all possible)?*

It is always a compliment to the recipient when the presenter knows something about them. It is more interesting for the audience to know a little history surrounding the award. Everyone loves to listen to a special story or anecdote about the winner.

Insight
Find out what the award is for and why they are receiving it.

SAMPLE SPEECH FOR THE PRESENTATION OF AN AWARD

This example can be made to fit more or less any award ceremony. It can be adapted to both leisure and business awards.

Insight
Make sure you get names and titles correct – ask beforehand.

Here someone has won an award for the best swimmer in their team.

- *Begin with where they were – When and where did they start? What made them interested in this activity? What motivated them?*
- *Go on to how they got here – What special achievements can you mention? Can you weave in some little stories? How can you bring in other events and show how they progressed?*

Remember to tell any amusing stories to bring it alive.
Include a couple of surprising statistics or facts but not
too many.

▶ *Then celebrate where they are now – What personal or*
amusing story can you tell about their achievement? Ask
friends and family to help you for personal insights. Give
a brief history about the award.

**They have now won this special award for... and this is how they
did it...**

Finish with:

**Many congratulations (name of winner) on your remarkable
achievement from (members of XX club/your team/all of us here/
your friends and family).**

If you are asking someone else to hand over the award, close your
presentation as described above with:

**I would now like to ask (name of presenter) to come forward to
present (name of winner) with this special award.**

The person/celebrity does not need to say anything except,
'Congratulations on your achievement.' They should smile, shake
hands with the winner and then hand over the award **face up and
towards** the recipient.

Top tips

▶ *Beware of inviting the winner up too soon. It is awkward to*
stand and wait while someone speaks about you.
▶ *It is easier (even if you are left-handed) to hold the award in*
your left hand and shake hands with your right. Make eye
contact with the winner and smile.
▶ *Make sure you can pronounce the winner's name – practise*
beforehand.

- So that the audience can see the presentation and/or take photos, hold the handshake for a little longer and both face the audience.
- Make sure the award is upright, signed and visible. Hold it a little higher than usual when handing it over.
- Be sincere and allow the presentation to focus on the winner and their achievement. This is their day; your role is to make it memorable for them.

Receiving an award

It is usual for the recipient to say a few words of thanks. In this instance the presenter and person handing over the award should step aside. As the winner leaves the stage the presenter should shake hands with the winner and lead the applause.

Accepting an award gracefully is like giving advice – you don't mind doing it but you are not interested in hearing it. Why is that do you think?

You've all heard the acceptance speeches on the TV at the various award ceremonies. There are very few who really stand out as meaningful or entertaining. With a little thought these moments could be both. The usual self-congratulatory remarks should be avoided: 'I'd like to thank my agent for making me a success, I'd like to thank my parents for my success and all of you for helping me to be a success...' It is much nicer to say simply: 'There are many people who deserve this award as much as I do, it's just that today it happens to be my turn.'

Winning an award or a prize for a job well done is a thrilling experience. If the award is accepted briefly with sincere enthusiasm it can be memorable for both recipient and audience. Here are some top tips to keep your acceptance speech appropriate and graceful.

Top tips

- ▶ *Keep it short and to the point – maximum 30 seconds unless agreed otherwise. Even then, one minute is the most an audience will generally listen.*
- ▶ *Think about what you can say to appreciate the praise you have received. Be as brief as possible (see examples below).*
- ▶ *'Thank you very much' is a full sentence. This is ideal if you are shy and don't want to linger.*
- ▶ *Keep a sense of humour – think of an appropriate quote or amusing remark to add to your thanks.*

Insight

When accepting an award, keep the thanks brief.

ALTERNATIVES TO THE HUMBLE 'THANK YOU'

- ▶ *'Today I have come top of the pile, but from here I've even further to fall.'*
- ▶ *'With this award I am apparently the best of the bunch – but as a bunch we make an even more formidable team.'*

Link humour to your role as an award winner

- ▶ *'I may have won the award for best goal scorer of the year – but my wife has given me the prize for the most holes in my socks.'*
- ▶ *'It gives me so much satisfaction to receive this award, particularly as I never won anything when I was younger except at a village fair. What was it for? The largest pumpkin in the allotment. This award beats that hands down.'*
- ▶ *'There are the "have-beens" and the "may-bes", but today I am one of the "have-nows". Many thanks.'*

13

Local clubs and groups

In this chapter you will learn:
- *how to get the audience's attention – and keep it*
- *how to use visuals to enhance 'dry' material*
- *about inspiring last lines.*

So this is it. You have been asked to speak at your local club or meeting and you have read in previous chapters about planning and preparation. You have seen that starting with real power is vital in getting the attention of your audience. You have learnt about beginning with metaphors, startling facts, unusual anecdotes and lively stories or quotes.

Note: It is useful to have read at least the first three chapters of this book before continuing. They are filled with useful tips and information for your success as a speaker. Chapters 1 and 3 also give advice on structure and strong openings.

Just like skiing down a snow-covered mountainside, preparation is vital for your safe passage down that slippery slope. So how are you going to capitalize on those 120 vital seconds where people are getting their first impressions? As you begin to speak the audience will be attentive and this is the moment to seize your chance.

Involving the audience

So how do you do the above? Every audience loves to be entertained, respected and involved. Ask yourself how you can involve your audience in those first vital 120 seconds. Here are some examples:

1 *You are speaking at a football club dinner. The audience is made up of football players and their wives. You have done some research and prepared the main body of your speech (see previous chapters). Whilst going through the archives you discovered a few little known facts about the club that people would be surprised to hear. Begin your speech with the words, 'Fellow members, wives and partners did you realize that…?'*
This immediately involves your audience and gets them interested.

2 *You have been asked to give a speech at your local book club. People are looking forward to the new book recommendations*

for the coming year. You have discovered that one of the authors used to live in your town. You have unearthed some fascinating stories about her life. Begin with, 'Fellow members, I have unearthed a remarkable story about a local author – you'll never guess who she is...'

From the word go the audience shares in your excitement and wants to hear more. You have 'hooked' them in and they are immediately involved.

3 *Try using a controversial statement to begin a speech. This would be appropriate for a presentation on global warming for example. 'I firmly believe that the planet will survive anything we throw at it, it is more a question of will human beings survive in the future.'*

Insight

Before speaking, select key people in the audience to make eye contact with.

LOSING YOUR AUDIENCE

There are other factors to be taken into account if you want to keep your audience on your side. The quickest way to lose your audience is if you:

▶ *start late or go over the allocated time*
▶ *are not prepared and your speech is unstructured*
▶ *have disorganized materials or equipment*
▶ *appear flustered and out of control.*

So practise the relaxation exercises in Chapter 2. Remember to breathe deeply from the diaphragm to steady your nerves. Make sure your equipment is working and organized – check it and then check it again just before you start!

Insight

It is vital to check your equipment and materials before you start.

How to grab your audience and keep them

During your research you may have found other interesting or humorous stories to weave into your speech. People relate to stories and in particular if they are accompanied by a visual of some kind. When preparing the speech to the book club in the above example, perhaps you could find an old picture or poster to show your audience that would bring that author to life. Use your imagination and use this example as a guide.

A financial advisor was giving a speech to a local business club. The members were aged between 27 and 55 years old. He started by saying,

> *Fellow members, today I have a question for you.*

He involved his audience straight away.

> *I would like you to think about how much money you are putting aside for your retirement on a regular basis.*

He then took out a balloon and began to blow it up slowly, stopping as he asked further questions.

> *How much have you put aside? This much?*

He blew air into the balloon.

> *This much?*

Another breath. When the balloon was over half full he continued,

> *I have several clients who have this much saved.*

He held up the half-full balloon.

> *Not bad, but not nearly enough to allow them to live as they do today. This is the amount you need.*

He blew the balloon up to its limit.

> **So, fellow members, how many of you have this much saved?**

He held up the full balloon so everyone was watching it. Then he took out a pin and popped the balloon making the whole audience jump.

> **But you have wasted all your money! The bubble has burst and you are left with nothing. It is almost too late, but not quite. My friends, I can help you, and this is how.**

What a wonderful example of how to grab an audience and keep it. The great visual made everyone remember the message and he was able to inspire his audience to act.

Personalizing your speech

One of the techniques used to 'hold' your audience is to personalize your speech. Speak to your audience as if the speech is only for them. If you are addressing an audience about recycling or 'green' issues, use a strong statement like: 'Every one of you in this room has at least 20 plastic bags in your home and most of you have over 50.' Or, if you are speaking at an international trade fair a question such as: 'Did you know that all of you are either wearing or have on your person at least five foreign products?'

Statements and questions keep your audience's attention and if you personalize them they will feel a direct connection with you, the speaker. Use a real world situation that connects to their club or organization. Audiences respond to seeing themselves in a given situation. This creates instant rapport.

Insight
Research and find a news item that will connect to your club or organization.

Another way to create rapport is to find out the names of some people in the audience and what they specifically came for. Later in the speech when you get to that part in particular you can look over to that person and throw in: 'Now this is what will interest you (name) as I know you are involved with/concerned by/etc....'

Top tips

Other ways to personalize your speech:

▶ *Use music as people arrive that you know they will enjoy (research again).*
▶ *Dress as your audience does – smart but not overpowering.*
▶ *Speak to your audience as they arrive and make them welcome.*
▶ *Create a conversational tone, your speech is not a performance.*
▶ *Smile now and then and stay relaxed, then they will.*
▶ *Move among the audience if at all possible and the space allows.*

Inspiring endings

Please also see Chapter 1 for inspiring final lines where strong openings and closures are covered in some detail.

As in your opening the conclusion is where you have an opportunity to leave your audience with a lasting positive impression.

If you posed a question at the beginning of your speech you may now reveal the answer. For example, at the trade fair above the question was: 'Did you know that most of you are either wearing or have on your person at least five foreign products?' During your speech this question may have been discussed but not revealed as the truth. You could involve your audience by asking them to finally check to see if this is the case. It is better, however, to demonstrate by using yourself, or someone you have asked previously, as an example. You could end by saying:

> *Finally I would like to remind you of the question I posed at the start of this speech. I asked if you knew that most of you would be wearing or have on their person at least five foreign products. I will now demonstrate with the help of [name]. In his breast pocket he has a pen made in Italy, a pack of tissues from France, and in an outside pocket he found a marker pen from Spain. He is wearing a jacket made in Hong Kong and his shirt is made in Taiwan. His shoes are made in Belgium and his tie was a present from the USA. As you can see he has more than five foreign products on his person. As you leave the hall/room you may like to see just how many items you have – you may just be surprised.*

You would then press home any point you were making in connection with this demonstration. This is a great way to finish as your audience will be thinking about the items as they leave and you will have made a real connection.

14

Fund-raising events

In this chapter you will learn:
- *how to be persuasive and motivational*
- *how to promote the benefits*
- *how to make a difference.*

Fund-raising can be a challenge. Usually you want to hook the audience by persuading them you have a worthy cause. Then, when you have them interested, encourage them to donate funds. This therefore is the occasion when the speech is certainly all about the audience and their reaction.

Getting action

So how do you persuade your audience to accept your reasoning and take action?

As you may know there are two sides to the brain. The reasoning logical side (left) and the imaginative emotional side (right). When people are making changes or accepting another point of view, they usually make decisions with the right (emotional) side and the logic comes later.

So what does this mean for the speaker?

Ideally you 'create' a picture in the minds of your audience. Allow them to visualize what it would be like. Explain in descriptive words and if possible evoke as many of the senses as possible.

Insight

It is important to help your audience to create a picture of what their money will fund.

EVOKE THE SENSES

If, for example, you are raising funds for a social club for the elderly, explain their current situation – no facilities, lack of stimulation, unable to get out of their homes and so on. Then paint a bright picture of how the club will support these vulnerable people. Use phrases such as:

> *Ladies and gentlemen* <u>*imagine how*</u> *this wonderful facility will look two years from now.* <u>*Picture the scene*</u> *– local transport will bring the elderly to the club and return them home. As they walk in they will see...*

and so on.

Then ask questions such as:

> <u>*How do you think people will feel*</u> *when they walk into the social club? Well, let's think about it for a moment,* <u>*what would we like*</u> *when we reach a certain age? What impact would the smell of a home-cooked meal have on someone who found it hard to cook at home? How much more pleasure would people with arthritis have when they don't have to struggle with heavy pots and pans?*

Then answer the questions:

> *This club will provide them with a sense of community. They will be able to make friends more easily... hot meals would be provided and people would feel supported instead of alone and vulnerable...*

Really allow people to have a clear picture of the end result. This will stimulate their imagination and enhance the success of your fundraising.

> **Top tip**
> People respond to new ideas when given small chunks of information, a bit at a time. Be careful not to cram too much into your presentation. Leave them in a state of anticipation and excitement. Then you will have the results you are looking for.

Considering your audience

Before you start your final presentation here are a few more questions to consider:

- ▶ *What facts or information do they need to hear that will move them to donate?*
- ▶ *How can you appeal to their emotions and their intellect?*
- ▶ *It is a good idea to weave stories into your factual presentation as 'people buy on emotion and justify with logic.'*
- ▶ *What stories can you tell that will have the greatest impact? If you can 'show' a story with props, PowerPoint slides or a DVD – all the better.*
- ▶ *What has worked well for you in past fund-raising events? Look at past successes and ask yourself what made people respond to you then.*
- ▶ *What can you find out about your audience in advance?*
- ▶ *Do they already know some facts and information? If so how can you surprise them? Gain as much knowledge as you can about your audience and then produce some facts and stories that will really grab their attention.*
- ▶ *Can you use testimonials or recommendations from respected individuals? If you have had donations from people your audience will respect, let them know. This may help to persuade them that your cause is worth supporting.*

> ▶ *What action do you want your audience to take at*
> *the end of your presentation? Be specific – give your*
> *audience precise information about how they can donate/*
> *participate.*

Imagine you were raising funds for a new youth centre. What
stories and anecdotes about the young people would appeal to
their emotions and their intellect? Help the audience to visualize
the benefits if they raised a specific sum of money. Show pictures
of the proposed new building at each stage and the costs involved.
If possible, find another new youth centre that has been a success.
Tell real-life stories about the benefits it has brought to the
community. Get your audience involved, ask them questions.
This will motivate your audience and persuade them to dig deep.
Ask one of the youngsters to come up and explain what it would
mean to him/her to have a new youth centre. Get excited by the
message and put energy into your presentation.

Insight

Use descriptive words to enable your audience to 'see' the
project.

Whatever your cause or topic, as you work on your research
find examples of how things have worked elsewhere. Invite
people you know the audience will respect and ask them to
reinforce your message. They can either speak in person or leave
a recorded message for you to play to your audience. Enhance
your credibility by using several sources to strengthen your cause.
This will help to make you more objective and add weight to
your message.

Ending with a bang

Finally end with a bang! People always remember what is said last
so keep building your presentation so that your strongest stories/
arguments/evidence comes at the end.

Don't forget to give very clear, specific information on how to get involved. People need to know how to donate, how to help with fund-raising and where to go for advice. Do you have leaflets you can give out with an easy form to fill in on the day? Perhaps you can give out envelopes or have a box where people can insert their cheques or cash. Can you set up facilities for accepting credit cards? Get them to take action on the day otherwise you may lose them.

Insight

Always end with a call to action. Be specific about what, when and where they can donate.

To summarize:

▶ *Begin with surprising information or a good story.*
▶ *Help people to visualize the benefits of the end result.*
▶ *Use phrases like 'Imagine what it would be like' or 'Think about how...'*
▶ *Motivate by giving examples of past success stories.*
▶ *Use visuals and testimonials to support your message.*
▶ *Involve your audience and learn about them beforehand.*
▶ *Build your message and create suspense.*
▶ *End with a powerful call to specific action.*

15

Giving a speech about your hobby

In this chapter you will learn:
- *how to tell interesting stories*
- *how to inject comedy*
- *how to demonstrate using props*
- *how to come up with surprise endings.*

In previous chapters you have read about how stories bring any speech or presentation alive. They create an instant rapport with your audience as most people relate to the emotions and enthusiasm of a real life story.

Think about why you decided to take up your hobby or activity; is there a story you could tell? What happened the very first time you took part? Did you make an amusing mistake or achieve a notable award or prize? Everyone loves to hear personal stories and amusing events that have happened along the way. It makes them feel involved, as they may have had a similar thing happen to them. If they can laugh with you about your incident this makes you closer to your audience and creates rapport.

Insight

Weave in amusing incidents and mistakes that your audience can relate to.

An example of this was when a guest speaker told of her embarrassment when skiing in the French Alps.

> *After skiing all morning, I was desperate to go to the loo and knew that there was a small restaurant at the bottom of the run. I hastily went in and struggled to remove my gloves and small rucksack. I then pulled down my all-in-one ski suit eventually reaching my thermal underwear. Feeling a great sense of relief, I suspended my bottom over the typical undignified hole in the ground. As I stood up, to my horror the small window to my left was almost level with the ground. Snow had fallen heavily and people had full view of my exposed rear. I was even quicker at getting out of there as I had been to get in, as you can imagine!*

Anyone who had been skiing in France could have identified with this incident. Her amusing but embarrassing story instantly endeared her to the audience. Everyone has stories to tell and when you tell your story you really don't need a script. They are yours and you experienced them first hand. You can tell them with heart and enthusiasm because they are your own personal experiences.

Speaking and showing

So what is your favourite hobby or leisure activity and how can you weave an interesting speech around it?

Some of the best speeches about hobbies and interests *show* as well as tell the audience about them. Take a speech about gardening, for example. It's inspirational to listen and watch someone demonstrating with several little pots and a trowel. At a local toastmasters' club Meg Hayworth had several cuttings laid out in front of her as she gave her speech and everyone could see exactly what was involved. At the end of her speech she invited the audience to come up and see the results. She involved all the senses of listening, watching, feeling and also smelling her new rose cuttings.

Another speech by the same member involved dog training. Yes, she actually brought her dog to the club and demonstrated exactly how she trained him. Of course if you use props or demonstrate your activity this takes the pressure off your actual words. People are focusing on what you are doing and many people find this kind of speech easier.

Insight

Take the attention off you by introducing props and demonstrations of your topic or hobby.

The three Ps (plan, prepare and practise) are very important for this kind of speech as everything needs to be assembled in the right place. You will need to place your props where they can be seen. If you are doing a demonstration you will need to lay everything out in advance and make sure each phase is set up in the right order.

Here are some planning questions to consider beforehand:

▶ *What hobby or activity would be best for my audience?*
▶ *How much do they already know?*
▶ *What would they like to see, hear, touch or smell?*
▶ *How can I bring my hobby or activity alive?*
▶ *What could I do to involve my audience in my speech?*
▶ *What do I know that would be new for them?*
▶ *Which interesting or surprising facts can I impart?*
▶ *Where will I assemble my props/items/PowerPoint?*
▶ *How can I ensure my audience goes away with something memorable?*
▶ *How long will this research and preparation take?*

So, now you have your ideas and you know what you are going to speak about. You have thought about some interesting facts and have planned a couple of stories to tell.

Insight

Introducing surprising facts and details your audience doesn't know can greatly enhance their interest.

Let's imagine you are speaking about the fascination of tracing your family history. This is very personal so how can you make it interesting for your audience? How much do they know about this topic? They may have heard about it but may not know how to go about it. Most people are interested in their family history but be aware that some people may be adopted or may not be comfortable with this subject. Research your audience so that the speech does not offend or leave anyone feeling left out.

Insight

Research your audience so as to avoid embarrassment.

Although this hobby is personal to you, ask yourself the questions above. If you think your audience would be interested in hearing about how you started, begin your speech there. Weave in ways to find out information so that they can start this journey themselves. Tell them about the mistakes you made or false avenues you went down before your were successful. If there are any humorous moments make sure you include them. Bring the speech alive by asking if anyone else has traced their family history.

Questioning your audience

Use questions that invite participation but not lengthy answers. For example, use closed questions (these invite a Yes/No answer):

▶ *'Have some of you here mapped your family tree? (Pause for replies.) Yes? It's very rewarding isn't it?' Or 'No? Well, I can really recommend it.'*

Using rhetorical questions is also an effective way to engage your audience (questions where replies are not really needed):

▶ *'I expect some of you here have also found out about your family history?'*
▶ *'Perhaps some of you feel that this is hard work? Not at all...'*

► *'Did you know that more than 20,000 people have used this website to carry out research over the past two months? Amazing isn't it?'*

Insight

Using rhetorical questions is a great way to involve your audience.

Using adjuncts

When tracing your family history, for example, perhaps there are websites or books that were particularly helpful to you. These could be made available in a handout or on a flipchart. You could show pictures of your ancestors or mementos you have collected. While telling a story about one of your family you could play music of that era. You could also pass around a photo or portrait for the audience to see and touch. Think about which props would amuse or interest people and begin to assemble them. Clothes, shoes and accessories, old record players with music and old-fashioned items from the period will all add spice to your speech.

Refer to Chapters 1, 2 and 3 to make an outline of your speech. Use startling facts, relevant quotes and stories to begin and end with a bang.

SAMPLE SPEECH ON THE TOPIC OF GARDENING

I hate gardening! (Unusual opening as this is the topic!)

I suppose you are all wondering why I am here at all? (Involving the audience and asking a rhetorical question.)

Well, (pause) there is one aspect of gardening that I have found to be wonderfully creative and rewarding. It's creative because I make the decisions about colour and foliage. I can imagine how my pots will look when completed and I can create little works of art right outside my back door. Years ago I made the decision to pave my small garden to save all the hassle of mowing, weeding and digging. I bought some lovely bright colourful pots and here are some smaller versions (she points to the pots assembled in front of her). I decided to create my own garden in pots and unusual containers (she holds up an old boot and a small kettle).

This speaker then went on to tell her audience how she used cuttings to plant up all her pots and containers. She allowed her audience to see clearly how the cuttings were made and which compost to use. She passed her little pots around so that people could really see the result. She also brought in large coloured pictures of the pots when in full bloom to inspire people. One pot had herbs that had already grown and she got the audience smelling and handling the herbs for themselves.

Her final words were:

Over the past two years I have saved a total of £560 by taking cuttings and creating my own garden (interesting fact). I no longer go to expensive garden centres and I use as much recycled material as I can. I make my own compost in an easy to manage container. Now, (pause while she searches for something) there's a small bag of it here somewhere – would anyone like a sniff? (An amusing ending to round off her speech.)

Being professional

When talking about a hobby, interest or something where you are an assumed expert, it is necessary to be credible.

People will judge you on a variety of areas:

▶ *your knowledge and expertise*
▶ *personal experience*
▶ *the way you plan, prepare and present*
▶ *your appearance and style*

- ▶ *your enthusiasm for your subject*
- ▶ *the way you project authenticity.*

To make sure you are professional and well thought of give some explanation of why you have the right to speak about this topic. Give them a brief idea of your experience and tell personal stories. When speaking and using props be enthusiastic and spontaneous. Show that you really care about what you are describing. This draws your audience in and makes them feel involved.

Be yourself – this is easily said but if you can be natural and easy with your delivery your audience will relax and enjoy themselves. Speak with conviction and energy.

Top tip
Try to look at a place on the floor or stage where you will be speaking. Create a fizzy spot that you can step into and feel that fizz and energy as it rises. Use that energy to create enthusiasm for your topic. Put a particular emphasis on certain key words to inject life and sparkle.

PUTTING THEORY INTO PRACTICE

Let's have a look at what this looks like in context. Look at the various hobbies and activities listed below with the emphasis shown in some sentences. Try speaking these lines out loud to get a feel for the sound and phrasing.

Mountain biking (could also be for skiing/snowboarding/mountaineering)
'What an **exhilarating** feeling after **finally** reaching to the top, to feel the wind **rush past** as you make your **daring descent** down the mountainside. There's **nothing** quite like it.'

Stamp collecting (could also be used for researching family history)
'This **fascinating hobby** allows you to get a **real insight** into other cultures and countries. The time spent researching and gathering data is **definitely** worth it. Not only do you have a sense of **achievement** but also something to pass on to **generations to come**.'

Flower arranging

'Every arrangement I make is like painting a **unique** picture.
I imagine the completed arrangement in my mind as a **beautiful** image. Each one **totally individual**, each one a **colourful** memory to **cherish**.'

Ceramics, sculpture, woodwork

'When I am **totally absorbed** in creating something, I forget what is going on around me. It is the **greatest** stress buster I know. Being able to see the finished article and realize you have **created it from scratch** is a **fantastic** feeling.'

All team sports

'Playing as part of a **team** and feeling the **support** of your colleagues is **great**. You are all striving to achieve the **same objective** as one. The sense of **achievement** and **pride** when you **win** a match is **amazing**.'

When you have crafted your speech and are happy with the content, leave them with a really memorable ending. Perhaps you can wow the audience with an unusual fact. Did your hobby or interest get a special mention in the press or on TV? Is there a celebrity who is connected with your topic? Perhaps you can come up with an unusual quote to end on.

You may have been asked to speak as someone who is particularly knowledgeable or a bit of an expert on a topic. It may have got around that you are someone who is an expert on wine. Alternatively, you may have a lot of knowledge of art history. In this case you will need to be a credible expert and finishing with a surprising fact or statistic is a good idea.

Here are some quotes to end this chapter:

▶ *'Don't talk about golf if you don't know which caddy to hit the ball with.'* (A. Lamkin)
▶ *'If you are going to talk about horses make sure you know your bits from your girth.'*
▶ *'Research and perception improve your reception.'*

10 THINGS TO REMEMBER

1 *Always ask yourself what topics would suit your audience.*

2 *Consider the etiquette if speaking at a formal dinner. The usual order of a speech is: compliments, amusing anecdote, toast.*

3 *Start with a bang (joke, quote, fact, amusing story). Get people smiling and laughing with you.*

4 *When thanking people, find something special to say about each person.*

5 *If a gift is involved, always plan where, when and how this will be handed over. Decide in advance whether a handshake or kiss is appropriate.*

6 *When speaking about yourself or your hobby, personal stories that reveal your own vulnerability can be very effective.*

7 *At a prize ceremony, find out as much as possible about the recipient.*

8 *Keep the awards in front of you. Hold the award with your left hand and shake hands with your right.*

9 *At a retirement event, maintain a positive tone. End with a little humour or special dedication.*

10 *At a fund-raising event, be clear about how, where and when people can donate. Make your call to action upbeat and passionate.*

Part four

Getting yourself heard

16

Networking events

In this chapter you will learn:
- *the key to listening*
- *the 60-second introduction*
- *how to ask useful questions*
- *how to sell the benefits*.

Networking is all about meeting new people and really listening to them. You are also letting them meet you so they can learn more about you and your business/work/life.

Top tip

In order to be a successful networker it is *more* important to be *interested* in them as well as you being interesting.

The key to listening

When you ask someone a question about themselves listen to their 'feelings'. Really hear where their pain is. Do not jump in with 'Oh yes, I know how that feels; I...' (this is your story but they want you to hear theirs). Your own stories can be told later in the relationship to create empathy. When you are networking with people for a short time it is important to learn about *them*.

So how do you listen for feelings? Here are some examples:

At a networking meeting a colleague who is a financial advisor asked how he could listen and then appeal to people's emotions when his job is so factual. So, let's think about where the issues are when we speak to someone in finance – worry about pensions, confusion about how to manage money online, frustration with mortgage providers, the list is endless. So, if you hear that someone has one of these issues listen carefully and ask a couple of specific questions, 'What have you done about this so far?', 'Is there anything else about this that is worrying you?'

Then, when you have listened carefully to the information – tell a story.

Insight

Asking questions initially is more appropriate than telling people about yourself.

Top tip

Avoid: 'Well, what you need to do is X' or, 'Well, my advice is Y'.

Instead, tell a story of the elderly lady you helped with her pension, or explain how one of your clients managed to get a great mortgage that saved them X amount of money. This will bring it alive for your listeners. It will appeal to their emotions and they will remember you. The empathetic networker listens with the intent to understand what is really on people's minds. Then they tell a short story to illustrate how they can solve the problem. In brief:

1 *Find the pain/issue.*
2 *Ask about it and really listen.*
3 *Tell a brief story to solve it/ease it.*

People who feel heard and understood will be far more responsive to any product or service you are offering.

Insight

Listen to people's stories and descriptions and you will learn how to approach them.

In his book *The Road Less Travelled*, M. Scott Peck writes:

> *An essential part of true listening is the discipline of setting aside one's own prejudices, frames of reference and desires so as to experience the speaker's world from the inside.*

Becoming a confident networker

So, how do you introduce yourself when entering a room full of people you have never met? Firstly face your fears and practise throwing out those voices that say:

▶ *I can't stand rejection.*
▶ *I don't want people to think I'm pushy.*
▶ *I can't just go up to someone and speak.*
▶ *I never know what to say.*

Really take hold of these thoughts in your hand and throw them in the bin. It is hard to change a thought pattern. They become comfortable habits. If you want to be a successful networker you need to practise getting rid of all those negative phrases and replace them with positive affirmations.

Insight

Ask questions to find out more about your colleagues and what they offer. Have one or two phrases ready when approaching people you don't know.

If you repeat the following daily you will become a more confident networker:

- ▶ *'I move on if someone is impolite and I don't take it personally.'*
- ▶ *'I have a confident attitude.'*
- ▶ *'I listen well and ask questions.'*
- ▶ *'I have phrases ready when I approach people.'*
- ▶ *'I tell stories and interesting anecdotes if requested.'*
- ▶ *'I learn from my mistakes and improve each time.'*
- ▶ *'I walk away with several contacts to call at the end of my meetings.'*

The 60-second introduction

Remember, you will never get anyone saying 'No' when you ask to join a group. Remember they want to meet new people too – that's why they're there.

Here are some phrases/questions to get you started as you approach a group:

- ▶ *'Good morning, may I join you?'*
- ▶ *'Excuse me, may I join in? I'm new here/this is my first meeting.'*
- ▶ *'My name's... (put out your hand and they will respond).'*

As part of the group, take time to really listen and show interest in their answers:

- ▶ *'How did you get started in your business?'*
- ▶ *'What makes it enjoyable?'*
- ▶ *'What areas of your business do you want to develop/are you working on?'*
- ▶ *'What changes have you seen in recent years that affect your business?'*

▶ *'How should I describe to others what you do?'*
▶ *'What makes you different from others?'*

This is a way to find out about other people and to collect their business cards. It is extremely useful to ask for their cards as then you can contact them later.

The 'elevator speech'

If people ask what you do, how do you answer them in 60 seconds or less?

Which answer gives people more information about you? 'I work in HR at Emass International', or 'Emass is a large media company. I'm the one that people come to with their concerns or questions about career advancement or training needs.'

Or which of these would you rather hear? 'I sell wiggets for Regant', or 'You know those really useful thin, black, plastic cable ties – well I sell those to all the big supermarkets worldwide.'

Insight
Make your own message powerful, persuasive and punchy.

When someone asks you 'What line of business are you in?' or 'What do you do?'

Try answering following this format:

1 *'Well you know when... (describe how people feel/think).'*
2 *'And then people... (describe the pain or suffering).'*
3 *'Well I... (solve the pain or discomfort).'*
4 *'So that... (tell them the benefits).'*

Here are some examples: (20–30 seconds)

Well you know when people are confused about which utilities they should buy or switch to? And then they spend hours searching for the right providers and getting frustrated. Well

> *I run a company that solves all that by selecting the right utilities for them every time. So that when they have answered a few questions I am able to get the very best deal for them possible.*

and

> *Well you know when people are planning a wedding and feel really nervous about giving a speech? And then they spend hours agonizing about it? Well I specialize in writing lively wedding speeches for every occasion and helping people to present them, so that everyone has a great time and no one needs to worry.*

Concentrate on the benefits you can provide rather than describing the product or service. Which is better at a networking event and which on an advertising board?

1 *'This is a great little lamp. It has an expandable stand and it comes in four colours. There are three modern designs that would suit any room in the house.'*

   or

2 *'Don't you think people always need a handy little lamp near their bed or on a sideboard? It's great to be able to adjust your lamp to suit your height isn't it? These lamps do all that and you can choose the colour and design you like to match your furnishings.'*

THE FIVE Ps

Many networking meetings like Business Networking International (BNI) or local enterprise breakfast meetings require participants to stand up and give a 60-second presentation of their business or service. This is a one-off chance to show the real benefits of your business and you need to take full advantage of this. So let's look at the five Ps of the 'One Minute Memorable Moment'.

Do:

1 *Plan your presentation to fit 60 seconds exactly.*
2 *Prepare your points (max 3) well.*
3 *Practise your presentation.*
4 *Prepare props or visuals.*
5 *Promote the benefits.*

Make your message the 3 Ps:

1 *Powerful.*
2 *Persuasive.*
3 *Punchy.*

Dos and don'ts

Important points to remember during the 'One Minute Memorable Moment'.

VOICE

▶ *Do vary your voice tone, volume and pace, to add more interest and prevent it from becoming a boring monologue.*
▶ *Do make sure that your voice is loud enough so that the person furthest from you can hear you clearly. Breathing exercises in Chapter 2 can help with this.*
▶ *DO NOT start while standing up or finish while sitting down. Stand up, then begin speaking. Finish, pause, then sit down.*

BODY LANGUAGE

▶ *Do make your body language positive, e.g. eye contact, posture, and facial expression. Each conveys a message about you and your service.*

- ▶ *Do stand up straight and be reasonably still as this suggests you and your message are solid and trustworthy.*
- ▶ *Do make eye contact with at least half the people in the room to increase their interest. Pick out those with friendly faces or those you know.*

MESSAGE

- ▶ *Do take time to say your name and your business objectives clearly and slowly both when you stand up and when you sit down.*
- ▶ *Do use all of the 60 seconds – if you only use 40 you are wasting your money.*
- ▶ *Do be specific: 'I'd like an introduction to the MD of JoBloges and Co.' or 'A good referral for me is an MD of a medium-sized IT company.'*
- ▶ *Do get a strap line that everyone will remember, for example: 'I'm the coach you can approach' (business/life coach); 'Making the world smile' (dentist); 'Getting your business noticed' (sign and notices company); 'I trim your figures' (accountant).*
- ▶ *Do tell stories of your successes. Tell them about a client and how you helped them. Tell them tips about things they would like to hear, not what you want them to hear. Don't ever tell them the same thing twice!*
- ▶ *Do try to be upbeat and enthusiastic. There's a big difference between 'Good morning' and 'GOOD MORNING'. (Robin Williams's 'Gooooood Mooorrrrrrrning Vietnam' may have been just a bit OTT, but it got attention.)*
- ▶ *Do ask for referrals, and be specific about the type you want, asking 'Who do you know who...?' The more specific the request, the more likely it will trigger a response in your listeners' heads.*
- ▶ *DO NOT ask 'Do you know someone who...' or 'Is there anyone you know in the XY industry?' The 'someone', 'anyone' sentences equal **no one!***

▶ *DO NOT cram too many points into your 60 seconds, they will all get lost in the verbiage. As they said in 1984, 'Less is more, more is less.'*

Holding your nerve

Remember, most people have nerves, however calm they may appear to others. So do take a few deep breaths before starting (the extra oxygen will stimulate your brain). Do start with enthusiasm and a smile. Do prepare and arrive ahead of time and do plan and practise as this will reduce nerves.

Insight
Try to arrive in good time and practise staying calm and in control.

If you are asked to do a ten-minute presentation all of the above apply. But during the ten-minute presentation don't think about it as ten minutes. It is only two minutes for the introduction, five minutes for the main points and three minutes for the conclusion. Use the time at the end for feedback and questions.

Prepare any handouts and give them out at the end, not during the speech – you want them to look at you and listen!

PRACTISE – SPEAKERS' CLUBS

If any of this seems daunting then join a speakers' club. These days there is usually at least one International Toastmasters' Speakers' Club in every major city in the UK. Here you can practise and get valuable feedback in a really safe environment. It will cost you less than £100 a year and you will learn so much more than speaking skills. Try it, it has helped many people to speak confidently in public.

17

Standing up for your rights

In this chapter you will learn:
- *how to be sure of your facts*
- *how to breathe and stay calm*
- *about assertiveness versus aggression*
- *how to give strong examples.*

At some time or other it will be necessary for you to stand up for
your rights. This can be a fairly routine event or campaigning on
a more significant issue.

You may need to have a discussion with your local education
authority about the choice of school for your children. You may
need to counter a proposal for a road running past your property.
You may even feel strongly enough about an issue such as climate
change, to be invited to speak about it in public. Whatever the
occasion you need to be armed with accurate facts and figures.
Your research will need to be meticulous and your three Ps –
planning, preparation and practise have to be second to none.

Have you ever heard a really convincing speech? Perhaps you
heard a good politician when he or she was passionate about the
future of the country under his or her leadership. You may have
heard someone like Winston Churchill on the radio or Tony Blair
when he first came to power. Winston Churchill was both eloquent
and passionate and gave some of the most memorable speeches

in British history. He once said that for every minute he spoke he would prepare and practise for an hour.

Many people asked him how it was that he could, apparently, ad lib during his speeches. He replied that there was only one way – to practise then practise and then practise again. Being spontaneous is only possible if you are well rehearsed, as every actor knows. Tony Blair also knew that preparation was vital and he was very practised at pacing his speeches. He was a master at using silence and pauses to create suspense and keep people guessing.

Insight

If you have something to say, mix this strong belief with sincerity.

The most convincing speakers are those who blend strong beliefs with authenticity and sincerity. Martin Luther King demonstrated this when he began his now famous speech 'I have a dream...'

This is a particularly relevant quote taken from his speech – The Strength To Love, 1963:

> *The ultimate measure of a man is not where he stands in moments of comfort and convenience but where he stands at times of challenge and controversy.*

Insight

Always present your views by backing them up with key facts and information.

Whatever your situation

It is not only famous speakers who are able to challenge people and/or express strong views. At speakers' clubs all over the world many people from different walks of life are standing up and practising for a variety of occasions.

Take this example:

A young man stood up to speak at his local club and began, 'I am a recovering drug addict and I believe that this club does a great deal to support people like me.' He was totally honest in his delivery and had very strong views on how society treats people with depression. He had done plenty of research into the causes of depression and presented the audience with relevant facts to back up his views.

Another example was a young woman who had discovered that her insurance company had made a serious error when handling a claim. She had called the company concerned but had been fobbed off with excuses. Her mentor at the speakers' club suggested she 'rehearse' the argument she wanted to present to the manager, in front of the club members. She planned out what she would say with all the relevant dates and documents and then presented it at the club. She got useful constructive feedback and advice. This gave her the confidence she needed to confront this issue and resolve it.

So when standing up for your rights as a public speaker you must:

▶ *do detailed research*
▶ *order your facts and data*
▶ *deliver with passion and energy*
▶ *create a genuine and personal connection with your audience*
▶ *remain calm and in control.*

In Chapter 13 we talked about how to be persuasive and to convince people. In this chapter you will also be applying the relaxation and breathing techniques discussed in Chapter 2.

It is necessary to stay calm in a situation where you are expressing strong views and may be affected by emotions. If you haven't yet read the first three chapters now is a good time to go through them before continuing.

Assertion versus aggression

Note: Please glance through Chapters 5 and 9 on handling hecklers before continuing.

Imagine the scene: you are feeling calm and prepared; your speech is well researched and you have delivered the introduction. You have just made an important point when someone calls out 'Hey, what's that again, I strongly disagree!'

> **Insight**
> If you hear comments or opposing views, please remember it is not usually personal. Keep to the facts.

There is no way you can control how your audience reacts to your speech. People may object; they may talk when you are speaking and they may leave the room. The most important thing to remember is this: provided you have done your research well and you are confident of your facts, such comments are not about you or your material. There are not many occasions when you will be disrupted but being forewarned is being forearmed.

Other people may react aggressively to such outbursts, but the key is *you don't*. First, allow yourself to take on other opinions. You are not there to *force* others to change their point of view only to request that they listen and reflect. Take a deep breath and understand that while you are on the platform you need to take charge of the situation without feeling threatened. Keep a firm steady voice and maintain eye contact.

> **Insight**
> If you are challenged, remain calm and in command of the stage.

So, what do you say when someone challenges you as in the situation above?

Try these examples:

- ► *'Yes, you have a right to disagree – perhaps we'll come back to that later.' Then quickly move on.*
- ► *'You are quite entitled to your opinion. I am just putting forward my own views and I have done a great deal of research.' Then you continue.*
- ► *'I hear that you have a different opinion and I would be happy to discuss this after I have finished my speech.' Smile and continue.*
- ► *Look around and get your audience's attention: 'I am sure we would all be interested to hear your views at the end of my presentation – at the moment it's my turn.' Then you continue.*

It is very useful to stop and consider just who these supposedly 'difficult people' are. As a matter of fact they are just like you or me but at this time they are feeling anxious, hurt or frustrated. They may feel powerless to express their opinion and this comes out more aggressively in the heat of the moment then they had intended. It is always up to you and your attitude and demeanour in a situation like this. If you stay in control, speak with authority and remain calm but firm, you will win through. It is up to you whether or not you allow one person to disrupt your speech. There will always be the typical 'know-it-all' and the eager 'must-get-a-word-in' or the sarcastic 'you-must-be-joking' types. It is they who have the problem and are seeking attention or a sense of personal worth. Keep in mind that most people will want to hear what you have to say, so keep your cool and stay focused. Above all, do not take the disturbance personally or let it affect your delivery.

TAKE PREVENTATIVE ACTION

Of course, prevention is better than cure so do make sure of the following:

- ► *Know who your audience is and how much they know about your topic.*
- ► *Give your audience time to relax and create rapport by introducing yourself to some individual members before your speech.*

- *Listen to their views and concerns and adapt your speech accordingly.*
- *Get your facts right and stick to what you know best.*
- *Keep the momentum and stay motivated.*
- *Remain focused and in control of your emotions.*
- *Examine your reactions and work at staying calm and respectful.*

Insight

After any challenge, breathe, pause and then continue.

Here is a great technique from the writer Judi Bailey. She has this advice when someone shouts out a comment and unsettles you: 'Imagine that the comment is a gust of wind and all you have to do is step aside and let it blow right past you. If you actually take that step to the right or left you feel more in control.'

Another tip from the trainer Ruth Dover is to imagine you are standing on a very bright red spot on the floor. This is your fizzy, motivated spot. If you have a disruptive person, just step back onto the blue, calm, in-control spot, to gather your thoughts. Once you have taken a breath, step back into the red spot again and take charge.

Top tips

In order to be an assertive speaker without aggression follow these tips:

- *Understand others and allow for the fact that people have different opinions – do you need to be right or do you want to be respected?*
- *Other people have needs and desires that we cannot always meet – that's OK.*
- *Maintain a firm and steady voice when faced with aggression.*
- *Stand firm and keep eye contact initially. (However, when continuing your speech look away to disengage.)*
- *Breathe deeply at least twice before answering any comments.*
- *Use positive language that shows the other person respect (even if they do not show it to you – model who you are).*

(Contd)

▸ *Do not take any comments personally.*
▸ *Allow any disruptive or aggressive remarks to 'blow' past you.*

Insight

Ask yourself this question: 'Do I want to be right or respected?'

Emotive facts, not fiction

When you are giving a speech that involves standing up for your rights or views you need to speak with conviction. You need strong arguments to back up your facts.

If you want people to take action use active speech. For example, 'What *we need to do* is to fight this cause for our children and grandchildren, *we need to* make sure that *we sign* these petitions today.' If however it is someone else who needs to take action you use passive speech. For example, 'This is vital to the business going forward. Voices *need to be raised* in protest at what is happening and members *need to be persuaded* to halt this unrest or we will be faced with disaster.'

Here are a few phrases you can try when putting forward strong views:

▸ *'It is my firm belief that...'*
▸ *'I hear what others are saying, however it is my strong desire to...'*
▸ *'If we look at the clear facts of this case we can see that...'*
▸ *'Not only is there... but also...'*
▸ *'It is out of the question to assume that...'*
▸ *'I am absolutely convinced that...'*
▸ *'I urge you to...'*
▸ *'Urgent action needs to be taken...'*
▸ *'People's lives are at risk unless we take action.'*
▸ *'I am sure you agree that...'*

- *'Research tells us that...'*
- *'In my opinion things need to change...'*
- *'This is what we need to do, right now...'*
- *'Unless we take action on this today, all will be lost.'*

NEGATIVE INVERSIONS FOR EXTRA IMPETUS

The use of negative inversions always adds weight to any argument as demonstrated by Winston Churchill when remembering the brave air crew in the Second World War:

Never has so much been owed by so many to so few.

Other examples of negative inversions for emphasis are:

- *'Not only do we need to address the issue of X but we also can't ignore Y.'*
- *'Never have I seen such suffering as in those towns I visited at the end of the trip.'*

Finally, you need to consider the actions that you want people to take as a result of your speech. Perhaps all you need is for them to listen, take in the facts and reflect on the information. Whatever you decide, clarity is key. Ask yourself what result you want and what, if anything, people should be doing or acting on. If you want people to sign a petition make sure it is available at the back of the room and direct people to it. Perhaps you have assistants who will collect signatures or funds. If there are handouts for people to take away, make sure they are available and easy to see.

If you have another event ensure people know about it and have the correct information.

Please remember that most people are there to have a good time and are not out to trap you. If you keep these tips in mind you will look forward to these opportunities to express your views. You have the right to stand up for your beliefs. If you keep your cool and speak with sincerity you will easily overcome any disruptions that may occur.

18

Preparing for an interview

In this chapter you will learn:
- *the importance of research*
- *how to create your own questions*
- *how to give yourself the edge.*

Interviews vary and the format can change from informal to very formal. They can last for one hour or between one and three days depending on the company or organization.

There are three key areas to consider wherever your interview is being held:

1 *The company or organization.*
2 *You as the candidate.*
3 *The interview itself.*

The company

It is useful to remember the following key points:

- ▶ *Always research as much as you can about the company before you go for an interview.*
- ▶ *Gather some knowledge of their products or services.*

- *Obtain and research the company's sales brochures and see if you can get hold of the company 'in-house' magazines or newsletters.*
- *Ask for a detailed job description.*

Insight

Never attend an interview unprepared – research and planning are key to success.

The candidate

The way you conduct yourself during an interview is crucial. Here are some common concerns facing candidates with suggested answers.

How do you announce yourself as you enter the room?

- *'Hello, my name is (your name) and I am here for an interview with (name of the company or interviewer).'*
- *'Good morning/afternoon, my name is (your name) – pleased to meet you.'*

What do you say if you are asked a question and don't know the answer?

- *'I am afraid I don't know but I am willing to ... (insert what is appropriate).'*
- *'I haven't had any experience of that but I am sure I could learn.'*
- *'I haven't come across that before, could you explain please?'*
- *'I don't know the answer to that I'm afraid, could you clarify?'*
- *'I'm not sure I understand you correctly, do you mean...?'*
- *'I'm not sure I know the answer so could you expand on that for me please?'*
- *'I'm sorry I don't know.'*

Bear in mind that it is always better to say you don't know than to bluff your way through. You will always be found out in the end.

What do you say when leaving the interview?

▶ *'Thank you for this opportunity, I look forward to hearing from you.'*
▶ *'Thank you very much, it was nice meeting you.'*

Even if you feel the interview did not go very well, keep your head up, your voice steady and thank them as you leave.

What to say when facing the interview panel:

▶ *Say why you want the job and tell them what your strengths are: 'I am very interested in (an aspect of the job) and I feel that my strengths as a (mention your particular strength/skill) will make a useful contribution to this role.'*
▶ *Let them know specifically what you have achieved to date in a similar role (if relevant): 'In my previous job I was particularly good at ... (your strengths in a team or during a specific task).'*
▶ *Express your personal and professional goals and values. Speak openly and honestly about them and what plans you have to achieve them: 'I would love to achieve my goal of ... (team leader) and I enjoy supporting others and seeing them grow. I feel this role would allow me to extend my communication skills and build on my existing qualifications.'*
▶ *Explain that you can provide references if required: 'I have two or three up-to-date references, and my referees are happy to be contacted.'*

The interview

For the presentation note down the key points you want to include. These may be (among others):

▶ *your knowledge of the company (brief overview) – two minutes*
▶ *how and why you would fit into the organization – one minute*

▶ *your particular strengths and experience with examples – five minutes.*

(Timing will need to be checked but the above is a general guide.)

If you have worked for this type of company before what experience will you be bringing to this role? Be very clear and specific. If this is a new role what transferable skills do you have? Often a role outside of work can contribute to your knowledge and skills. It is very useful for companies to hear about *all* your experience, knowledge and skills, not just role-related skills.

PREPARING YOUR QUESTIONS

Top tip

Remember the key points from previous chapters:

▶ *Your voice tone and body language are very important.*
▶ *Speak clearly and keep eye contact.*
▶ *Breathe and listen carefully to the responses to your questions.*

Think about what you need to know and practise delivering all the questions you can think of. Base your questions on your research and knowledge of the company. Overleaf are just some examples to guide you. They will not always be appropriate for your interview but will give you a general idea.

Before the interview, ensure any thoughts that are interfering with you being totally focused, drift out of the window (traffic, disagreements, problems, work and so on). Focus on your preparation and bring yourself fully into the room. Notice what is going on around you and show interest.

Insight

Make a list of questions they may ask you before preparing yours.

Concentrate on your deep breathing to keep calm – one breath out to release the tension, one breath in to gain energy. Use your breathing techniques to steady your nerves. Give yourself some positive affirmations before entering the room. Remember these are positive statements in the present such as:

- *'I am well prepared and have my questions ready.'*
- *'I have sufficient knowledge and skills to do this job.'*
- *'I am able to remain focused and relaxed.'*
- *'I can learn what I don't know.'*
- *'I am smart and suitably dressed for the role.'*
- *'I keep good eye contact and sit upright.'*
- *'I answer questions with due consideration and enthusiasm.'*
- *'I feel confident and know I can do well.'*

Here are some general questions you may like to ask during your interview:

- *'How many people are employed in this section/department/area/company?'*
- *'Do the teams/employees work collaboratively?'*
- *'How are employees supported?'*
- *'Do you have a high turnover of staff?'*
- *'What gives you the edge over your competitors?'*
- *'What makes this a good company/firm/organization to work for?'*
- *'Do you supply a uniform (if appropriate)?'*
- *'What hours will I be required to work (if these are not in the terms and conditions)?'*
- *'Do you supply meals or vouchers?'*
- *'Who will I be reporting to? Who is my supervisor/manager/boss?'*
- *'What holidays am I entitled to?'*
- *'What salary can I expect to receive?'*
- *'How is this paid?'*
- *'Is there a bonus system?'*
- *'Will I be working on commission or for a salary?' (Some sales jobs are based on commission, so check this out.)*

Now begin to formulize your own questions. What do you need to know about this company/job? What are the key areas you'd like to hear about?

After looking through your own questions put about ten of them in order of priority and get rid of the rest.

THEIR QUESTIONS

It is important to think about how to deal positively with any challenging questions that you may be posed during the interview, such as:

- 'What do you know about the company and its products/ services?'
- 'That's interesting, can you expand on that?'
- 'In your CV you mention you have experience in X. How would you apply your experience to this role?'
- 'Tell me more about your knowledge of X?'
- 'What makes you particularly suited for this job?'
- 'What past experience and skills can you bring to this job?'
- 'What are your main strengths and weaknesses?'
- 'How do you see yourself in this role?'
- 'What attracts you to this job?'
- 'There will be a lot of (travelling/stress/teamwork etc.) involved – how will you deal with that?'

There are many different questions that can be used in job interviews. This book does not attempt to provide all of them. Instead, you will gain an understanding of the type of questions that determine successful interviews. These will also prompt your own questions and help you to prepare for them in advance.

When you know the kind of questions you will be asked it is easier to prepare. This is a sure way to give yourself the edge over the competition.

What made you apply for this job?

If you have researched well and you know specifically what interested you in this position, this question will be straightforward. You may answer: 'Well, although this is my first job I was very interested in X.' If possible also say why you were interested. If you have experience or knowledge of the job you can answer: 'Well, as I used to work in X this job is ideal. I have skills and knowledge in Y and I really enjoyed doing Z in my previous job.'

Even if the job is boring, not exactly what you wanted, or if you are not particularly interested, try to remain positive and enthusiastic. It is always your attitude as well as your aptitude that will determine the outcome of your interview.

How good are your organizational skills?

When you first read about this role you may have thought that you had no organizational skills at all. However, everyone has organized something in their lives. Look at your hobbies and interests to see what you have organized. Maybe you were part of a team but you still had a role to play in making that event or situation successful. Dig deep and find what you have done in your personal and professional life to add value to your interview responses.

If you have very little experience stay truthful as it never pays to lie at interviews. Your answer could be something like: 'My organizational skills have not been tested too much. I have been helping my local club with their fund-raising events though, and I am able to manage my own time quite well.'

Find something you are good at and let the interviewer know, even if you feel it is not very significant. It may make all the difference.

What have been your most successful achievements to date?

Again, you may think your achievements are not worth mentioning. Remember to think positive. This is your chance to show the interviewer what you can do.

You may have won a prize: 'Well, last year I won an award for the presentation I gave to our regional teams.'

Were you a member of a successful team or organization? What hobbies or interests do you have? You may have done something for charity: 'Actually I belong to a local charity and I do their books for them and help them organize events.'

In your working life what positions have you held and what responsibilities have you taken on?

Insight
Practise speaking clearly, breathing and staying calm.

MORE ADVANCED INTERVIEWS

Applying for a position where you will be managing other people or taking on a leadership role may need other considerations. Often you will be asked to attend a whole day interview and give a short presentation. Questions may arise to test your personal style or personality.

James is one of many servicemen who have recently retired from active service. He wanted to use his many skills in an interesting and challenging position. Having worked for the Air Force, he decided to apply for a job with one of the civilian airlines as a pilot. He was asked to attend an interview lasting all day.

The first part was an interview in front of a panel. The second was a scenario-based interview assessing leadership and decision-making skills. Finally, there was a group interview where candidates had to give a speech lasting for between five and seven minutes.

During the day James was mingling with other candidates and senior company employees. He had studied the company background and was fairly sure they were looking for outgoing people who would be able to interact well with their customers. James made sure that he spoke to

(Contd)

as many of the candidates as possible. He made a real effort to create rapport with individuals and applied his listening skills to good effect. During the panel interview he had prepared relevant questions and his extensive research enabled him to answer their questions.

For the group interview candidates were given two questions to think about during the day.

1 *If you could have lunch with three people living or dead, who would you choose and why?*
2 *What made you choose this airline to work for?*

At the end of the day all candidates were asked to give their answers to the questions in a speech lasting between five and seven minutes. This was in front of all the other candidates and senior employees. James applied all the public speaking techniques he had learned as a member of a Toastmasters' speakers' group (see Chapters 1, 2 and 3).

He had only a little time to plan but made a few notes as the day progressed. He used the following techniques to help him in his presentation:

▶ *Breathing and relaxation techniques as in Chapter 2.*
▶ *He made sure he was passionate and enthusiastic by thinking positively.*
▶ *He had a strong statement for his beginning.*
▶ *He told interesting stories about the people he had chosen to join him for lunch.*
▶ *He put in some dramatic pauses.*
▶ *He made sure he kept eye contact with his audience.*

His research into the airline had given him plenty of reasons why he wanted to work for them. This gave him confidence when answering the second question.

Needless to say James received the offer of a job a few days later. He was thrilled.

At these all-day interviews you can see how extensive research plays a vital part. Also displaying confidence and mingling with people you have only just met is extremely important. Finally, the experience gained from speaking in public was invaluable.

If you refer back to the *first three chapters of this book*, there is no reason why you too should not be successful.

Plan, prepare and practise. You are ready – now go for it!

19

....

Speaking effectively on the telephone

In this chapter you will learn:
- *how to listen without judgement*
- *how to create rapport*
- *how to ask relevant questions to gain all the details.*

Communicating effectively

You may feel that using the telephone is not one of your favourite pastimes. You may like the telephone but come away feeling frustrated at not having got your message across. Perhaps you work closely with others in a team and need to have effective communication throughout the company. You may need to answer enquiries and deal with customers/clients on a daily basis. In each of these situations and in many more you need to be able to:

- ▶ *listen without judgement*
- ▶ *create rapport*
- ▶ *make a connection*
- ▶ *be aware and attentive*
- ▶ *be natural and authentic*

- ask relevant questions
- treat others with respect
- help them find the information and resources to reach solutions that are right for them
- be confident and assertive.

If you are communicating effectively you will:

- Create the right impression and give out positive signals: 'Good morning/afternoon how can I help you', 'This is XY company, Jane speaking, how can I help', 'Good morning I am calling to speak to Mr/Ms X is this a convenient time?'
- Feel confident about your own abilities: 'Yes, I can help you with that…', 'I'm sorry I am not sure, let me put you through to X who will be able to help you', 'Mr X is not available at the moment, can I ask him to call you back?'
- Be able to deal with conflict and difficult situations effectively: 'Yes I am aware of that and we are working hard to resolve the situation', 'I apologize for any misunderstanding, what exactly was the complaint?'
- Feel in control and be proactive: 'Yes, I will pass this on to our technical department and they will contact you by the end of today', 'Of course we would be happy to refund you the money by the end of this week.'
- Create excellent results for both yourself and your clients/staff/team.

This is an opportunity to extend your communication skills. It will enable you to think about the way you handle telephone calls and deal with people remotely. By understanding the elements above you gain choices, confidence and greater empathy within all relationships.

Insight

If possible, prepare for the call in advance by writing questions and key facts.

Active listening

Listening is about hearing what *is* said, not what you *think* is being said. As you prepare to listen, think about being non-judgemental. Be respectful of other people's reality, views and culture. When you are actively listening you are sensitive to the context; you clarify, affirm and summarize.

Insight
Always repeat the main points back to clarify what you have heard.

Let's explore the three levels of listening, which are:

▶ *superficial*
▶ *active*
▶ *deep*.

SUPERFICIAL LISTENING

You can all listen while at the same time doing other tasks or thinking about your own experiences: 'Oh yes I remember when I did the same...'

You are listening with half an ear or with your own story or ideas, ready to jump in at the earliest possible moment.

ACTIVE LISTENING

You are listening at a deeper level. The speaker is holding your attention and you use words such as, 'Really', 'Yes, I see', 'Oh yes, certainly.'

You show the speaker you are interested and attentive.

DEEP LISTENING

Here you are totally focused on the speaker and the content of what they are saying. There is no chatter in your head and you are not anxious to jump in with ideas, stories or suggestions. You allow the space for the other person to speak. Even if they pause you remain silent or prompt with 'Did you want to say/ask anything else about that?'

To delve deeper for further information or to get clarity ask questions such as:

▶ *'What specifically did you mean by...?'*
▶ *'Can you give an example?'*
▶ *'What exactly do you expect from...?'*
▶ *'What exactly do you mean when you say X...?'*
▶ *'I have a clearer picture of this issue now, how would you like to proceed?'*
▶ *'I notice you are concerned about... how can I help you?'*
▶ *'If I did X or Y would this solve the issue?'*

Once again, listen at a deep level to the answers and stay positive and solution-focused. If people feel 'heard' they are more likely to respond well to any suggestions you make.

Insight
Listen carefully for key facts and information.

Top tips
▶ *Listen well.*
▶ *Reflect back what you hear: 'So what you are saying is that you... Is that correct?', 'I heard you say that X is the issue/problem/situation, is that right?'*
▶ *Clarify and summarize: 'I heard you say that... What do you mean exactly?', 'Can you be specific?', 'Could you clarify that*
(Contd)

please?', 'Would you mind repeating that please, I'm not quite clear?'
▶ *Then give suggestions/solutions/ways forward.*

Creating rapport

Rapport comes from showing someone, through behaviour or words, that you understand and respect the way they see the world. It isn't about agreeing with someone, it's about putting them at ease. You can then build a relationship of trust by being genuine and fully present whilst on the telephone.

Insight
Remember to sound respectful even if you do not feel it.

Examples of rapport include:

▶ *Building trust by being consistent in your actions and behaviours.*
▶ *Acknowledging how it is for someone, perhaps by commenting non-judgementally on their current state: 'I understand your concerns and I will do the best I can to address them', 'This has obviously been an ongoing problem. I can help you with this.'*
▶ *Remembering what's important to another person: 'You have explained your requirements exactly and I will do what I can to help.'*
▶ *Being able to empathize with another's viewpoint: 'Yes, I see what you mean. Perhaps we can start by...', 'I accept that this situation is unsatisfactory. Let's consider the options.'*

Rapport is particularly important when you want to put others at ease. It can help you to promote a better relationship between yourself and others. This deepens the trust between you and your customer. Rapport can help people know you are on their side. It is especially useful when you disagree with someone's view and want to maintain a good relationship with them. Or, when someone seems ill at ease – anxious, hostile, frightened or lacking in confidence. It also helps when you want to encourage someone to confide in you or say more.

MAINTAINING RAPPORT THROUGH PACING AND LEADING

When talking to people notice their pace and tone. Speak a little faster if they are fast, slow down if they speak slowly. Keep your tone similar to theirs; not mimicking but being sensitive to the rise and fall of their voice. Pacing means you're going to be taking your lead from them… *subtly!* By talking their kind of language you will enable them to feel comfortable and at ease.

Note: Treat pacing with awareness as this can result in you or the person feeling ridiculed/embarrassed if overdone.

Without pacing, all we are doing is telling people things, giving them orders or responding to information. Pacing is a powerful way of connecting with someone and showing them respect. If we gain trust and respect we can offer someone new choices they are more likely to find acceptable.

If a customer is feeling unhappy and says, 'I am so frustrated with the poor service I have received', rather than trying to cheer them up too soon, try matching their energy level. Talk quietly but firmly as they did. You could say, 'Yes I can hear your frustration and am really sorry you had this experience'. Only then do you start to lead them out of their state by gradually becoming more positive. Raise the tone and volume of your voice and make suggestions to help solve the problem: 'I'd like to find out exactly what has happened here. Then we can try and put this right. Let's go over the details?'

Telling someone to 'calm down,' or that 'everything will be fine' is a sure way of increasing their unease. If they feel that you are empathizing with the situation they will be more agreeable to any solutions you come up with. Being in rapport is not the same as agreeing with them. You can still disagree and have rapport.

Questioning skills

When you are genuinely curious, you are no longer in the role of expert and you are meeting the customer half way. Even when your goal is to persuade, you can't do that effectively without first knowing your listener's concerns and objections.

There are a variety of questions for different purposes:

▶ *Information gathering or open questions (what, why, when, which, how, who)*
   'What kind of course were you looking for?'
   'Which advertisement are you referring to?'
   'Whom did you speak to last time?'

▶ *Closed or directive questions*
   'Have you got the postcode please?'
   'Did you phone on Monday last?'
   'I'll see what I can do today and call you back, is that OK?'
   'That one seems to meet your requirements; shall I place an order?'

▶ *Helpful questions*
   'Is there anything else we can help you with?'
   'How can we solve this issue for you quickly?'

▶ *Challenging questions*
   'How can we bring this to a satisfactory conclusion?'
   'Can you give me specific details of the call and the person you spoke to?'

▶ *Assertive questions*
   'I have done all I can at present. Will you be in tomorrow? I can call you back then.'
   'I see your point, leave it with me to sort out. When would be convenient for me to call you back?'

Phraseology

Below are some useful phrases used in the various stages of a telephone call. These are general examples you can adapt to suit.

▶ *Answering a call*
Note: *State the name of the company and then your name* clearly *and* slowly.
'Language Trainers, Marianne speaking, how may I help you?'
'Upton & Perks Ltd, Nick here, how can I help?'

▶ *Passing a call to someone else*
'Just a moment, please. I'll see if she/he's available.'
'Putting you through now, please hold.'
'I'm sorry she/he's not available just now. Can I take a message?'
'I may be able to help you?'

▶ *Asking someone to 'hold on'*
'Please hold the line, this won't take a moment.'
'Please hold on, I'll check that for you.'
Note: *Never ask someone to 'hang on' – it is impolite.*

▶ *Asking for more info/personal details*
'I just need a few more details please...'
'Can I take your name and contact details please?'

▶ *Requesting spelling and clarification*
'I'm sorry I didn't get that/catch that. Can you repeat it for me please?'
'I'm not sure I understood you correctly was that...(repeat the details)?'
'Can I just clarify that. You requested...(repeat details)?'
'Please can you spell that for me?' (You should be familiar with the alpha beta system.)

▶ *Taking a message for someone else*
'Yes certainly, I'll give him/her your message as soon as she/
he gets in. Can I have your contact details please? And the
message you'd like me to pass on?'
'Would you like her/him to call you back?'
'When should she/he get back to you? When would be
convenient?'

▶ *Dealing with a complaint*
Note: It would be useful to read the section on creating
rapport on page 190. Also, remember that people are
not necessarily angry with you so there is no need to take
comments personally. Stay detached and focus on finding a
solution for the customer.
Do not be intimidated and stay calm but firm. Keep pace and
tone to match the client's but do not raise your voice quite as
high if the client is angry.
Other phrases you could use might include:
'This is very unsatisfactory. Please let me see what I can do.'
'I am sorry you have been inconvenienced. I would like to
resolve this and find a solution for you if I can.'
'If we go through the details together perhaps we can find
a solution.'
'Let me take some details and get back to you this afternoon.'

▶ *Getting your point across*
'Yes I see/hear/understand your point, and (not BUT) I just
need to clarify…'
'I think that under these circumstances I must request
immediate payment/refund/action.'
'I have passed your comments on to my manager. I will ensure
you are contacted by the end of the week.'
'Leave this with me and I will call you back by the end of
tomorrow.'
(Always give people a time or day when you will return their
call/complete an action. 'As soon as possible' is meaningless.)

20

Making an initial enquiry

In this chapter you will learn:
- **to know what you want and write it down**
- **how to self-speak**
- **about body language.**

Enquiries you may wish to make may include:

▶ *Asking about an adult education course.*
▶ *Booking your car in for an MOT.*
▶ *Checking your travel arrangements when going on holiday.*
▶ *Booking or changing a hairdressing appointment.*
▶ *Enquiring about your bank statement.*
▶ *Finding a local dentist, doctor or health centre.*
▶ *Renewing your insurance and checking the details.*
▶ *Finding out about the local events in your area.*
▶ *Asking about local schools for your children.*
▶ *Checking details of a product or service you require.*

Picking up the phone to enquire about a service, product or course can be daunting. Going along to an unfamiliar place to make an initial enquiry can be quite intimidating for many people. Thoughts may go through your head such as: 'What shall I say exactly?', 'Will I sound stupid?', 'What will they think of me?'

Insight
Write down the key facts and information you need to know and then formulate your questions.

Facing your fear

It may be interesting for you to know that science has traced these fears back to a vital part of the brain called the amygdala. According to Daniel Goleman, author of excellent books on emotional and social intelligence, some people have a lower threshold of fear than others. It is by all accounts a genetic trait. The good news is that anyone can overcome these fears if they are supported and given encouragement. So if you face your fears and work with the methods in this book you will become more confident. You know that every time you attempt something new, be it taking an unfamiliar journey or learning a different language, small fears creep in: 'Will I get lost?', 'How will the weather affect my journey?' and 'Will others learn faster than me?', 'Can I cope with all these new words and phrases?'

However, with practice and constant repetition you achieve success despite your initial doubts. The fourth time you make an initial enquiry is much easier than the first and after the sixth time you wonder why you were so hard on yourself.

It is helpful to block out those negative voices before picking up the phone. If you are meeting face-to-face give yourself positive thoughts and focus on the other people and the enquiry you are making. Tell yourself you will overcome your fears and smile – even if you feel nervous.

Insight
Always use positive affirmations before you make your enquiry, to allay any fears you may have.

DON'T FORGET THE THREE Ps

Once again, as in previous chapters, careful planning and preparation is key. First, write down what you want to know. For example, if you are enquiring about taking your car for an MOT you may need to know:

- ▶ *when they can carry out the MOT*
- ▶ *if they have experience with your type of car*
- ▶ *what documents they need from you*
- ▶ *the cost*
- ▶ *if they provide any additional services.*

Then you write the actual questions in the order you want to ask them. If necessary, have the questions beside you when you phone. If the enquiry is face-to-face then rehearse the questions before you arrive.

Use positive thoughts before making your enquiry such as:

- ▶ *'I will be able to ask these questions as I have planned and prepared well.'*
- ▶ *'I am able to speak clearly and calmly.'*
- ▶ *'I will remember to breathe.'*
- ▶ *'I have read the section on assertiveness and am prepared.'*
- ▶ *'The more I practise the better I will become.'*
- ▶ *'When I have made two enquiries I will be more confident.'*

Here's an example of an enquiry. If you are enquiring about taking an evening course at a local education centre once again ask yourself what you want to know, for example:

- ▶ *'What days and times is the course being held?'*
- ▶ *'How long is the course for?'*
- ▶ *'What levels are available?'*
- ▶ *'What qualification does the teacher have?'*

- ▶ *'Is this an exam course?'*
- ▶ *'Is a course book provided?'*
- ▶ *'Will I get a certificate on completion?'*
- ▶ *'What are the fees?'*

You may be asked some questions too so be prepared for:

- ▶ *'This course is fully booked, would you be able to come on another day/time?'*
- ▶ *'Have you ever taken a course in this language before?'*
- ▶ *'Are you a beginner?'*
- ▶ *'This is an exam course, is that what you are looking for?'*
- ▶ *'How would you like to pay?'*
- ▶ *'Can you come to the centre to register or can you register online?'*

If you do the research beforehand by getting details of courses, times and dates you will reduce the number of questions you need to ask.

Insight

Do your research beforehand on the internet or at a library, as this can greatly reduce anxiety.

Body language

When dealing with people face-to-face body language can be even more important than the words you use. Just imagine the last time you spoke to someone who was depressed and feeling low. They probably looked down and had their shoulders slumped. They did not stand tall and they affected the way you felt too. Think about the last time you spoke to someone who was really enthusiastic about something. You may have noticed that they looked you in the eye. They may have made gestures and were holding their head up and standing tall. Enthusiasm is infectious and you can

be drawn into the positive feelings of the other person without
realizing it.

Insight

When you meet face-to-face, keep your body upright and use
good eye contact.

Imagine yourself in front of the bank manager asking for an
overdraft. If you approach him or her with your shoulders slumped
and give little or no eye contact, what impression do you think
he will have of you? Will you give him or her the confidence in
you? Do you think you will receive your overdraft? Even if your
words are positive your body is saying you really don't expect to be
successful.

Insight

Remember that people need to feel confidence in you before
they will agree to your request.

Imagine greeting the bank manager with a firm handshake and
good eye contact. Visualize yourself walking with your head held
high and shoulders back. Make an attempt to smile and show
that this is a person to be trusted. Then if you have prepared your
questions and essential information well in advance you will get
the result you want.

21

Making a complaint/confronting authority

In this chapter you will learn:
- *how to get down the key facts*
- *how to feel comfortable with assertive behaviour*
- *how to use the 'I' message*
- *how to get the results you want.*

It would be useful to read the previous two chapters on telephoning skills and making an initial enquiry, as they are also relevant.

Everyone has made a complaint or had to confront authority at some stage in their lives. In the UK people are actually less likely to complain than in many other European countries. We are regarded as quite a tolerant society in general and this can have both positive and negative consequences. On the one hand it is gratifying to be thought of as tolerant, on the other if no one complains then nothing improves. It is the way you complain that is the key to getting the results you want. Aggression and anger do nothing to endear you to others. It is best to leave the complaint until you have calmed down and can deal with things rationally. Sometimes easier said than done.

Insight
If you collect all the evidence and facts of the case beforehand, you will stand a better chance of getting good results.

Taking a step back before moving forwards

If at all possible, prepare well in advance. Get down the key facts and evidence before you confront people. You may be making a complaint about an issue, a situation, a mistake or about someone's behaviour.

If someone's behaviour is bugging you, get right to the point. Say what you have to say succinctly and then invite them to join you in a dialogue. Open the conversation tactfully and bear in mind the following points:

▶ *Be brief and clear about your position and your feelings.*
▶ *Make sure the person understands your thoughts.*
▶ *Find out if others share your views.*

Potentially volatile situations should be approached with caution. Think about the way you enter into the conversation, how you handle the conversation and how you reach the desired outcome.

Insight
It is useful to find out if other people share your views.

THE FIRST ENCOUNTER

The first thing to consider is the way in which you begin your conversation. Plan, prepare and practise just as you would for any speech in this book. Look at what you need to achieve, how you will resolve the issue and your ideal outcome. Then plan exactly what you would like to say as you begin the conversation. Mention specific behaviours or situations you found unacceptable and give examples. Tell people how you felt at the time and make it clear what is needed to resolve the situation. Allow others to give their side of the story and listen without interrupting. Be assertive but not aggressive by standing your ground and at the same time using positive language.

Below is a case study of a complaint to a bank manager.

A colleague was sure that his bank had made a mistake on his account. Initially he phoned to complain but was met with unhelpful customer service personnel. He decided to make an appointment to see his Business Manager. He prepared all the documentation and noted the times of his phone calls to the bank. Then he drafted his opening phrases making sure he had all the facts right. His opening was as follows:

> *Good morning Mrs Andrews. I have asked for this meeting to clarify what I consider is a mistake on my account (no accusation, but a clear deliberate statement). This mistake concerns the transfer of £1,500 from my savings account (number xxx) to my current account (number xxx) on 6 January this year (sticking to the facts). Regrettably this money is not showing on my account and has caused me a great deal of worry. I am now feeling extremely concerned as it is 20 January and the money is still not in my account. This is despite the obvious withdrawal of funds from my savings account (stating feelings and how this has affected him).*
>
> *I am hoping you can give me a satisfactory explanation (invites the bank manager to resolve the situation).*

If you are making a complaint about a situation that has arisen rather than the behaviour of an individual, many of the above points apply. You will need to be clear of your facts and do your research.

Insight
Using 'I' language to state your case is better than accusing people with 'You' (did this…, were that… etc.).

Another scenario might be that you booked a holiday that went wrong. When you arrived at your destination the hotel had not been fully completed and you were given rooms in a nearby hotel.

There was no direct access to the beach as you had been promised and the food and service was poor. Here, you need to locate the representative to lodge a complaint. Later, on your return, you would need to write to the company.

In this case the holiday representative is not directly responsible for the situation. They are only doing their job and as such can only take the details of your complaint and pass it on to the company. They are usually not very well trained and are working just for a short season.

When making any complaint it is advisable to ask yourself:

▶ *Who is directly responsible for the situation?*
▶ *What can be done immediately?*
▶ *What exactly are the facts of the case?*
▶ *What evidence can you provide to back up your complaint?*
▶ *What documentation will you need?*

Then consider your situation carefully before tackling the problem. You will seldom resolve a difficult situation with anger or aggressive behaviour. However, you will need to be assertive and sure of your ground.

In the case of the holiday above, here is an example of how to address the holiday representative stating briefly your feelings and the facts of the situation:

> *I am extremely unhappy about the hotel we have been allocated. My family is very disappointed, as we were promised direct access to the sea. We have to walk a long way to the beach and the food and service is poor.*

Decide what action you want the company to take and then say, for example:

> *I am not prepared to stay in this hotel and I would like you to offer us an alternative hotel that is near the sea and has a higher standard of food and service.*

This shows that you are not prepared to tolerate the situation and gives the holiday rep a possible solution. This may not be an option if all the hotels are full but it shows that you are not taking this situation lying down. Think through all the options that you would be prepared to accept. Then offer the holiday rep these suggestions as calmly as possible. If there is little response or you are met with resistance then here are a few questions/phrases to use:

▶ *'What exactly are you prepared to do about this situation?'*
▶ *'Are there no other alternative hotels you can suggest?'*
▶ *'Is there really nothing else you can suggest to improve this situation?'*
▶ *'I understand that there is nothing more you can do but I will be taking this up with the holiday company. Please provide me with all the necessary contact information.'*
▶ *'I will be taking this matter further on my return. I would like to take your full name please.'*

If the situation is so intolerable that you have decided to return immediately then you will need to make this clear to the holiday rep. Make it plain that you will be contacting the company and if possible ask the holiday rep to sign a document you have prepared outlining the facts of the situation. This can be used as evidence when you are asking for compensation on your return.

If you are making a complaint to the person directly responsible then you will be able to press your case more firmly. For example, after stating the facts of the situation you may say one of the following:

▶ *'The alternative hotel is not acceptable and my family and I will be leaving tomorrow. I will expect a full refund on my return.'*
▶ *'I am not able to accept this situation. I expect a full refund or an alternative holiday.'*
▶ *'This situation has become intolerable and I can accept nothing less than a full refund.'*

Avoiding accusations

The statements above can be used in a variety of situations by replacing the word 'holiday' with the item you are returning or the issue you are dealing with. Show respect for the other person and use a firm tone of voice when dealing with these issues. Keep eye contact and show that you are polite but not willing to back down. It is always more effective to use 'I' rather than 'You' when dealing with tricky situations. 'You' can seem accusing.

Compare the following examples:

▶ *'I am not prepared to accept this situation'* versus *'You make this situation unacceptable.'*
▶ *'I am very dissatisfied about the way this has been handled'* versus *'You have handled this badly and made me very dissatisfied.'*

Always state your own feelings and thoughts about the situation using 'I' messages where possible:

▶ *'This is the situation as I see/understand it'* versus *'You obviously don't see/understand what I mean.'*
▶ *'I don't share the same opinion and feel that my ideas are not being considered'* versus *'Your opinion is different and you are not considering my ideas.'*

Top tip
Using 'I' in these situations will enable the receiver to find a solution. If people feel accused they will be less likely to resolve the issue, or reach an agreement.

22

Taking part in a debate

In this chapter you will learn:
- *how to be the proposer*
- *how to be the opposer*
- *how to make speeches from the floor*
- *how to sum up effectively.*

Debating clubs and societies exist all over the world. Many people who now speak for a living started off as a member of a debating club. Schools and colleges hold competitions and it is an excellent way to hone your speaking skills. At universities there is always an active debating club. Many politicians learnt how to campaign and lobby during these lively discussions.

So, what exactly is a debate and how is it structured?

The purpose of a debate is to view and discuss all sides of an issue or topic. An example may be something from the local news such as whether or not to build a new car park on a disused site. Alternatively, it may be an issue where people are really passionate about a particular topic. One example could be whether we are doing enough to reduce our own carbon footprint. Another might be about changing the side of the road we drive on in the UK and if this would be feasible.

Chairing a debate

When you have decided what your topic will be this is called the motion. You as the 'proposer' would begin: 'I would like to propose the motion that... (and add your topic or issue).'

This topic is then debated and a vote is taken at the end. The point of view gaining the most votes is then 'passed' and the motion is 'carried'.

The motion is a carefully worded statement and one speaker will prepare a case in support of the 'proposer' while someone else will take a stance against it and support the 'opposer'.

This is the order for a typical debate:

1 *Main speaker proposes the motion – ten minutes.*
2 *Main speaker opposes the motion – ten minutes.*
3 *Second speaker supports the motion – five minutes.*
4 *Second speaker opposes the motion – five minutes.*
5 *Speakers from the 'floor' (other speakers wanting to make a short contribution).*
6 *Summing up by the main speaker opposing the motion – five minutes.*
7 *Summing up by the main speaker proposing the motion – five minutes.*

A chairperson runs the meeting and makes sure everyone gets a fair chance to speak. This person should:

- *be fair and not favour one side over another*
- *start by reading the prepared statement for the motion*
- *clarify the rules, timing and lights*
- *keep to time*
- *invite speakers from the floor*
- *ensure the debate flows effectively*
- *intervene when necessary if passions get high*
- *declare the votes 'in favour' and 'against', 'carried' or 'lost'*
- *be at all times friendly and good humoured.*

Proposing and opposing

Both main speakers get approximately ten minutes to set out their argument, starting with the proposer and followed by the opposer. After the main speeches the second speakers have a chance to support the motion and oppose it for five minutes each.

Insight
Do prepare your ideas in advance and research key facts.

If you are the main speaker proposing the motion it is important to work with your support speaker as a team. It is trying for the audience to have to listen to the same points twice. It is therefore necessary to discuss beforehand exactly what points you will both be covering. This applies equally well if you are the opposer.

After the main four speeches the debate is opened to all those in the audience (the 'floor'). Members and visitors alike are welcome to speak for up to three minutes on either side of the motion. When everyone who wants to has had their say, the main speakers will sum up their side of the motion for about five minutes each. By tradition the opposer goes first and the proposer has the last word before a vote is taken.

If you are answering some points raised by the proposer or the opposer you will need to make a few notes while he/she is speaking. As the opposer you may want to argue against the views of the speaker proposing the motion. This is fine as long as you remember to put across your own case at the same time!

Insight

Get plenty of different views and opinions on the subject from colleagues before you speak.

CONCLUDING

As the proposer you need to be very focused in the summing up phase. You will have heard several views and counter arguments and will need to put all these into a brief summary.

Top tips

▶ *Praise those who appear to be on your side.*

'Thank you for supporting my comments and giving some very valid points particularly... (mention a couple of key points they mentioned).'

▶ *Briefly counter any strong points made by the opposition.*

'I must strongly disagree with the points made by my opponent with regard to...'

'On the contrary it has been proved that...'

▶ *Sum up your main points strongly, emphasizing any areas that may have grabbed the audience's attention.*

'So to conclude I would like to state the main points which are...'

▶ *End on a particularly strong point and throw in a quote or startling statement.*

(Contd)

'I will end with a very relevant quote by... (one you prepared earlier).'

'Of course you will all know what was said on this subject only very recently and that is... (surprise them with a startling fact).'

Insight
Practise using your voice to best effect and sound confident by placing stress on key words or phrases.

Debating is not a public speaking competition and the audience is expected to cast their vote based on their views and the arguments put forward, *not* on the quality of the speeches. However, if the speaker is clear and convincing they are more likely to encourage people to vote for them! All the chapters in this book will help you to be a convincing speaker. Chapter 17 is particularly relevant if you are thinking about taking part in debates. Finally, it is extremely important that all speakers in a debate respect one another's views, even when they may disagree with them. The purpose is to enjoy the debate, hear different views and then abide by the vote.

10 THINGS TO REMEMBER

1 *Do not take challenges or questions personally. Stick to your facts and restate your view if necessary.*

2 *On the phone, keep your voice tone even and non-judgemental. Pace your voice where possible to that of the receiver/caller.*

3 *Ensure that you get all the information you need by repeating key information.*

4 *Remain calm and keep emotions out of the calls.*

5 *When complaining, make sure you are calm and in control. Be firm and avoid aggressive language. Use language beginning with 'I' rather than 'You'.*

6 *Be specific about what outcome you want. Give clear examples of poor service or behaviour.*

7 *Aim for a positive outcome or solution as far as possible.*

8 *Before an interview, research the company by visiting their website. Gain knowledge about their service or products.*

9 *Ask for a detailed job description in advance. Think about the questions they may ask you.*

10 *Focus on your strengths and key skills. Your attitude is as important as your aptitude.*

Part five

Speaking for business

23

Business meetings, arrivals and departures

In this chapter you will learn:
- *how to focus on the message required*
- *how to come across as professional*
- *how to use your voice effectively*
- *how to greet new employees and give farewell thanks.*

Addressing a business meeting

You have been asked to lead a business meeting. Your audience is not completely unknown to you but you may not be familiar with all of them. So how do you start to plan for this meeting?

For the sake of this example assume that your meeting will be held in the boardroom and there will be 12 people present. You are the communications manager in a very large company and on this occasion you will need to present dry factual information. (In previous chapters you will be able to pick up more about how to present dry material. However, in this example you can keep it as simple as possible.)

When planning ask yourself:

- ▶ *What do the attendees already know?*
- ▶ *What essential information do they need?*
- ▶ *How long will each point last?*
- ▶ *How can I present this information as clearly as possible?*
- ▶ *What has worked well in the past? (Or, not so well?)*
- ▶ *How can I weave in a human-interest element?*
- ▶ *Is there anything else I can do to enliven this material?*
- ▶ *How will I know that I have covered everything they need?*

If you are chairing the meeting you may need to ask further questions such as:

- ▶ *Who should attend?*
- ▶ *Who needs to be there for the entire meeting?*
- ▶ *When and where will it be held?*
- ▶ *What are the key objectives?*
- ▶ *What options may be suggested?*
- ▶ *What actions will be taken as a result?*
- ▶ *Who will be involved in these actions?*

Delegating

In both cases you will need to decide what planning and preparation you will be taking on and what you will delegate. Delegation needs to be clear and time taken to ensure this is done effectively will save you hours of hassle.

Delegation is highly effective when you have the following:

- *A positive and mutually involving working environment where your leadership style is democratic, consultative and participative.*
- *The willingness to put in sufficient time and effort to make delegation clear, with precise instructions enabling it to work effectively. For example: 'I would be grateful if you could find the results of X and the figures for Y and have them on my desk by the end of the week. You will be able to find this information in Z department. Thanks for your help.'*
- *The skill to use the greatest competences and abilities of your staff – usually in the planning, research and organization of your meetings and presentations.*
- *The confidence and trust in your team to complete delegated responsibilities and accomplish required activities. For example, 'This shouldn't be a problem for you but if you get into difficulties please let me know what you need.'*
- *The ability to motivate and inspire greater personal performance from your team and allow them to take responsibility: 'I understand that this is a new task for you but I feel confident that you will be able to carry it out. Do you have any questions? Is everything clear?'*
- *The skill to provide sufficient authority when you are delegating and to define and communicate the parameters of this authority: 'If any problems arise where you feel you are not able to make a decision please let me know immediately so we can discuss the best way to proceed.'*
- *The clear priorities and deadlines for completion of tasks and progress reports. For example, 'I need to have the results of X on my desk by the end of the week, the research for Y can wait until 26th at the latest. Please let me know if there are any likely delays.'*
- *The ability to relinquish control so that your direct reports take ownership of the tasks delegated and have the freedom to act and take decisions where appropriate. For example,*

> *'Have you understood all the elements of this task? Is there anything else you need to know to achieve this? If you need any help do you know whom to ask? Are you clear as to what is needed? Are the time scales adequate?'*

▶ *The ability to take calculated risks and reduce these by careful monitoring. Remember, delegate don't abdicate! For example, a few days later ask, 'How are things progressing? Will you be able to deliver this on time? Anything else you need? That's great, carry on you're doing fine.'*

Obviously you will be doing the delivery yourself and need to prepare and practise with the material. However, time can be saved if you delegate the research and organization of the meeting to your PA or secretary if you have one. This will free you up to organize and structure your presentation.

Focusing on the message

This seems obvious but it is often the case that meetings grow longer as people get sidetracked. Ask yourself how you can best stay on track and how you will bring things back to your main points. It is important to get the balance between allowing people to give their opinions and ideas while at the same time keeping to your agenda. If you find it useful, at the beginning of the meeting flag up your intention to leave ten minutes at the end for questions or ideas. If you do get sidetracked, here are a few phrases to use:

▶ *'Thanks for your input, I'd like to come back to that later.'*
▶ *'Great ideas, let's park those and discuss later.'*
▶ *'Perhaps we can discuss this further after the meeting/at the next meeting.'*
▶ *'I'd like to move things along now as we have a good deal to cover today.'*
▶ *'Thank you, I'd like to consider that later, let's move on.'*

The most important question to ask yourself is, 'How can I
stay on track?'

Professional considerations

In these types of meetings the priorities are different, remember the
following:

- ▶ *Be on time.*
- ▶ *Keep on track.*
- ▶ *Embrace ideas and suggestions.*
- ▶ *Motivate and listen to your audience.*
- ▶ *Ask key questions to get ownership and responsibility for actions.*
- ▶ *Get the required commitment and deadlines for actions.*

When asking your staff/team questions it is helpful if someone
writes key words on a flip chart. Here are some examples of the
kind of questions you could use:

Objectives
- ▶ *'What are our long or short-term objectives/goals?'*
- ▶ *'These are the objectives for the organization (state/write them).'*
- ▶ *'What goals do you/your team have – in line with our
  company goals?'*

The current situation
- ▶ *'How do we see the current situation?'*
- ▶ *'What is currently happening/in place?'*
- ▶ *'Where are we with X, Y, Z?'*

Choices
- ▶ *'What choices do we/you have?'*
- ▶ *'What are our/your strategies?'*
- ▶ *'What possibilities are available to us/you?'*
- ▶ *'Who else is involved?'*

Actions to take

▶ *'What actions will now be taken, when?'*
▶ *'Who will take responsibility for X, by when?'*
▶ *'What time frames have we set for our actions?'*

ENABLING YOUR TEAM

You will develop your own questions depending on your meeting and the agenda. This model enables your staff/the team to take responsibility for their own ideas. If you use questions to enable them to take ownership of the tasks, they will be motivated to carry them out. For example:

▶ *'This sounds like a good idea, what support do you need?'*
▶ *'Who else may be involved?'*
▶ *'What needs to happen now for you to take this forward?'*
▶ *'When can you have this completed by?'*
▶ *'Is there anything else you need?'*

Try to avoid imposing your own ideas too early on in this process as this will curb their creative thinking. If ideas arise that you find you are unable to accept, thank the staff for their input and explain your reasons clearly.

Insight

It can be very motivating for your staff if you listen to their views where possible and then act on them.

You will usually have a variety of different personal styles in any meeting room. There will be those who speak a lot and some who will listen and reflect. You will need to gently and tactfully stop the flow of conversation on occasions as explained above. In the latter case you may need to encourage those who have not contributed, for example, 'Bill, I would value your opinion on this', 'Amy, do you have anything to contribute?' It is often those who are quietly reflective who come up with the best ideas. They may not be the first to jump in but their silence may hold useful suggestions. Some companies also introduce a suggestion box for people to add their ideas and comments.

TIMEKEEPING

When closing the meeting ensure that all your points have been covered. Timing is crucial and people will not respect you if you run over. Check that everyone is clear and that their requests have been heard.

▶ *'Is everyone clear about their tasks/actions?'*
▶ *'Do you have all the information you need going forward?'*
▶ *'I have noted the following points, are they correct?'*
▶ *'If there are any points you need to discuss further, I am available at… (time/date).'*

Close with:

▶ *'Thank you for your useful contributions, our next meeting is… (time/date).'*
▶ *'Thank you everyone, I am grateful for your ideas/suggestions/input.'*
▶ *'Thank you for your attention and feedback.'*

THE PROFESSIONAL VOICE

When you stand tall and breathe from the diaphragm (see Chapter 2) you will achieve the best vocal production. If you are speaking to a large meeting, project your voice by speaking to a point on the back wall. See your voice bouncing off and when practising use your hand to grab your words and extend them out towards the wall. Pause and take a breath before a vital piece of information. Make a note of the words you want to emphasize. In order to put authority into your voice you need to lower your tone. Men are usually fine as their voices are lower but for women this can be vitally important.

If you feel your voice is a little high and you want to lower it for meetings and presentations try the following:

1 *Maintain your breathing from the diaphragm.*
2 *Make the sound 'uh ha' as if you were agreeing with someone. Notice where 'uh ha' is resonating in your chest.*
3 *Relax, breathe and hum at this pitch (this is your natural pitch).*
4 *Now hum a little lower, notice how this sounds (this is a little lower than your natural pitch but don't force it).*
5 *Try saying 'Good morning, welcome to the meeting' in your lower pitch.*
6 *Repeat this in your natural pitch and notice the difference.*
7 *Repeat in your lower pitch remembering to breathe and stay relaxed.*
8 *Now breathe and project in your new lower voice to the back wall.*

If you practise this you will develop an awareness of when your voice sounds lower. After a while you will be able to switch easily from one to the other. This will not happen immediately but with practice it will become more natural. Your vocal folds are very sensitive so use tepid water at meetings and do not overstrain your voice. If you feel you are straining then stop and resume later.

Insight
Use your voice effectively by lowering the tone, pausing to breathe and keeping calm.

Welcome speech to new employees

When preparing speeches to employees it is vital to set the right tone for the occasion. When welcoming new employees ask yourself the following:

▶ *What do I want them to know about the company?*
▶ *What particular points do I want to emphasize?*

- *How will I make it lively and interesting?*
- *How can I create a positive impression that inspires them to work well in their job?*
- *What key facts will I end with?*

These speeches do not usually last longer than 50 minutes, sometimes shorter. Plan and time your speech and then think through the above points. Once you know what your key points are, refer to previous chapters to inject enthusiasm and energy into the speech. Your aim is to inspire and reassure the employees that they have made a good choice. Include some interesting facts and figures and weave in personal stories of individual success. Remember the 'personal interest' when delivering dry material.

So how do you open your speech? Here are a few examples to get your own ideas flowing:

> **I am delighted to welcome you to** (company name), **we have been in operation for over 15 years and have an excellent track record in customer care. I remember a particular occasion when…** (relate a personal interest story to illustrate how a specific employee demonstrated a good example of customer care and the outcome).

Or

> **Welcome to** (company name). **It gives me great pleasure to announce to you our plans for the coming year** (you announce your plans). **I hope you will all enjoy working here and will come to us with your ideas and suggestions as to how we can improve and continue to grow.**

Farewell speech to leaving employees

People leave for a variety of reasons. They may have reached retirement age, they may be leaving as a result of ill health, or they may be moving on to a different company. You may have had to dismiss an employee, resulting in bad feeling. Whatever the reasons you need to consider the possible emotions of the person leaving. They may be feeling sad or redundant or pleased to be moving on. They may also be feeling aggrieved. The speech needs careful planning and it is always a good idea to speak to other colleagues to gauge the mood of the person leaving. This speech is usually no longer than about three to five minutes.

Ask yourself the following:

- *What positive achievements has this person contributed to the company? (There is usually something you can mention even if the person has been sacked.)*
- *Are there any amusing stories to tell that colleagues have contributed? (Not to cause embarrassment but to create a supportive mood.)*
- *Are there any particular workmates who would be willing to tell their own personal interest stories about this employee? (Negative comments to be avoided.)*
- *What specifically has this person contributed to the team as a whole?*
- *What would be an appropriate gift for the person leaving after a long service?*
- *How will you wish them well and thank them for their contribution?*
- *Is there a suitable quote that you could end on?*

Top tip

If you are presenting a gift, it would be better to leave this to someone else. You can then call them to the front and ask them to hand it over. This could be a good colleague or member of their team.

UNTIMELY DEPARTURES

If you are planning a speech for someone leaving 'under a cloud' you may choose not to make a speech at all. If you decide to do one keep it short and sincere.

Think about:

▶ *any truthful good points you can mention*
▶ *how you may admit the problems but not dwell on them*
▶ *the words you will use to close the speech.*

Here are a few examples to close your speech with sincerity.

For someone who has been sacked:

▶ *'Despite the problems we wish you well in your future position, and the very best of luck.'*
▶ *'We sincerely regret that this decision had to be taken and we wish you well for the future.'*

For someone who decided to leave after a conflict of opinion and take a new position elsewhere:

▶ *'Although we have had our differences we respect your decision to leave and wish you well for the future.'*

For someone who has been made redundant:

▶ *'These occasions are never easy for either side. We regret that things have turned out this way and wish you the very best of luck.'*

If you are sincere and do not hide the truth of the situation you will set the tone for a successful speech. Focus on the positive but do not overdo the praise and flattery. Pick out specific situations when people were successful or made useful contributions. Tell stories to illustrate events or particular accomplishments. Props and pictures can enliven the speech and add a touch of humour where appropriate.

Finally you will no doubt recall the following: KISS – keep it short and simple.

24

Business seminars

In this chapter you will learn:
- *how to distinguish between a presentation and a seminar*
- *how to plan the various elements*
- *how to answer challenging questions*
- *how to leave participants with actions.*

A business seminar is usually a form of instruction offered by a professional training company or expert speakers on a specific topic. It has the function of bringing together small groups for regular meetings, focusing on a particular subject. Generally, everyone present is requested to take an active part in the discussions.

This is often accomplished through an open forum with a seminar leader or instructor, or through a more formal presentation of results or research. Questions can be raised and sometimes debates are carried out. It is relatively informal when compared to a less interactive presentation or lecture.

Insight
As you will generally be leading an open forum, think about how to encourage participation and interaction.

As a speaker or subject expert, it is crucial to know your audience and do your research. In the UK many Enterprise Agencies hold regular seminars for start-up businesses. They know exactly what people are looking for when starting their business and run seminars on:

- *marketing and branding*
- *business planning*
- *financial planning*
- *information technology*
- *customer care*
- *employment law.*

The way people learn the best is when they hear it explained, have it demonstrated and then have a chance to experience it. In a seminar this is exactly what you are aiming for.

Seminar structure

There are often four main elements:

1 *The input of information.*
2 *The demonstration or presentation of findings.*
3 *The hands on participation, discussion or debate.*
4 *The possible further action points.*

If you were considering presenting a seminar on public speaking you would firstly find out about the experience of your audience. Is this the first time they will be speaking in public or are they coming for more advanced presentation skills? Once you know the level of expertise you can plan your structure.

Insight

Remember that you will be perceived as an expert and as such will need to do research and advance preparation.

In this seminar example on public speaking you could take some of the material from the first three chapters of this book. However, in a seminar you would involve the audience by giving a demonstration of the breathing and relaxation exercises and then asking them to have a try. In the next section you might give out information on various planning strategies. Following this you would invite your audience to discuss which strategy suited them best. You would encourage them to add their own ideas and solutions. This could be done in small groups or as one group depending on the size of your audience. By enabling the participants to break into small groups you are skillfully taking away the fear of having to present to a large group. They can get used to presenting their ideas without it feeling like public speaking. Finally, when they have finished their discussion you can invite one member to present the findings to the whole group. You will need to be sensitive and select one member who you feel will not be daunted by the prospect.

Insight
Always find out how much your audience already knows.

Ensuring participation

So, what kind of phrases would you need to encourage your audience to participate?

In this scenario you need to show enthusiasm and remain upbeat. Assume that everyone will participate and encourage them with phrases such as:

▶ *'Right, now it's your chance to have a go!'*
▶ *'You've now got a chance to try out your skills.'*
▶ *'The best way to learn new skills is to give it a try, so let's begin.'*

Be very clear what it is you want the participants to do and what result you are aiming for. If you are intending to select someone to give feedback from the group let them know in advance. Another way would be to allow the small groups to select someone as a spokesperson themselves.

Insight

It is a good idea to ask one group member to give the feedback.

When encouraging the small groups to give feedback you may say fairly assertively: 'OK, so now let's hear some ideas or strategies from each group. The group in the far corner, would you begin please?' or 'I'd like to keep to time so now let's get each group's feedback and ideas please.'

You do not need to spend more than a couple of minutes getting feedback from each group. Then move on to the open discussion or debate if appropriate.

Insight

Encourage participation by asking questions and dividing your audience into smaller groups.

QUESTION TIME

At this stage you may like to ask questions about the information you have presented so far. There may also be questions from the audience. It is always useful to consider in advance what questions may come up whatever your subject. Put yourself in the position of the participants. What would they ask in this situation? With the above example on public speaking they may ask:

▶ *'How do I get over my fear of drying up?'*
▶ *'What can I do to calm myself before a speech?'*
▶ *'I always speak too fast. How can I slow down?'*

Think about the possible questions that may come up and you will be ready for them as the hands are raised for your attention at the end. If you get questions that you are unable to answer, don't panic just take a deep breath and select from:

▶ *'If I understood you correctly you would like to know...?'*
▶ *'Just to clarify, was that...'* (Repeat the question back to clarify and give yourself time to think. This has the added bonus in that the audience can also think about it.)

- ▶ *'That's a great question, can I get back to you on that one at the end of the seminar?'*
- ▶ *'I like that question and it needs some thought, can I get back to you?'*
- ▶ *'That may need a little research on my part so let me take your e-mail.'*
- ▶ *'Well that's an interesting question, anyone like to answer that?'*

There is usually someone willing to try but if not you can always tell the truth if you're not sure and get back to them later. You do not need to be the expert all the time and people will warm to you if you are seen to be vulnerable. No audience likes a know-it-all and it gives them encouragement if they can answer a question for you. Likewise, if not everyone fully supports your ideas be open about receiving differences of opinion. Accept that not everyone at every seminar will agree and embrace the diversity of the audience. As a consequence you will earn the respect of your participants and peers.

Just remember, if you are in an open discussion ensure you do the following:

- ▶ *Allow for a variety of ideas and opinions.*
- ▶ *Speak with confidence and conviction.*
- ▶ *Frame your points logically.*
- ▶ *Back up your ideas with facts, diagrams and stories.*
- ▶ *Enrich your ideas with anecdotes and relevant quotes.*
- ▶ *Use encouraging language to get the audience to buy in.*

ENCOURAGING ACTION

At the end of the seminar after the question and answer session it is useful to get commitment to actions or follow-up. You could ask:

- ▶ *'So, as a result of today, I would like to go around the room and ask you what specific actions you are going to take.'*
- ▶ *'Perhaps you have been thinking of some action points to take away from today. Please be kind enough to share these with the group. Let's start with (name).'*

Or if there are no particular actions you could ask:

▶ *'Please let me know what one piece of information you found particularly helpful today. Let's start with (name).'*

Gaining feedback

Always use feedback forms as a way to find out how people responded to your seminar. If you don't ask your audience how well you performed you can't be sure if you succeeded or if you can repeat that success in the future. Seek out evidence of how well you did as it is the only way to improve your delivery.

One seminar I attended ended on a very unusual note and you may find this appeals to you. It encourages people, in a subtle way, to take action.

Place an unlit candle on a side table at the start of your seminar. As you draw to a close light the candle. Ask everyone to think very carefully about what they would like to do as a result of the information they have received. Then ask them to help you to extinguish the candle by thinking very hard about it collectively.

Pause to let them think for a minute. Of course the candle will not go out.

Then say: 'Thinking about what you will do is admirable but it is the action itself that makes it happen.' Then blow out the candle!

25

Speaking for international audiences

In this chapter you will learn:
- *how to spot communication roadblocks*
- *how to recognize the world view of others*
- *how to use words wisely.*

The influence of culture on communications is so strong that anthropologist Edward Hall once said, 'Culture is communication and communication is culture.' Differences in cultural values and perception can be an invisible source of misunderstanding between people from different regions. In this section, you will find various means and strategies of overcoming communication roadblocks arising out of cross-cultural differences in perception. To quote Professor Geert Hofsted, who has perhaps conducted one of the most comprehensive surveys on the subject, culture is nothing but 'The collective programming of the mind, which distinguishes one category of people from another.'

Insight
Watch out for cultural misunderstandings – do your research!

There are two types of problems in communicating with people across cultures. The first is the inability to note and read the symbols other cultures display. The second is the tendency to attach to the symbols meanings derived from one's own world view or culture. Take the simple example of two men holding hands or kissing each other ardently on both cheeks. This can be a very acceptable public behaviour between, say, Arabs or Russians, but not between Brits or Germans, where such a form of greeting might lead to embarrassment. What may be considered natural, appropriate and, therefore, welcome in one culture may be entirely unwelcome and even offensive in another.

Insight

Your body language and gestures can be more important than your words.

Negotiating

In *Negotiation and Conflict Resolution*, Dr Yang says that, 'We must consider the impact of situational factors and negotiating tactics, while predicting the basic outcome of a negotiation process.'

For this he recommends that managers must do the following:

- ▶ *Analyse the difference between intra-cultural and cross-cultural negations.*
- ▶ *Discuss the role of culture in the conflict resolution process.*
- ▶ *Appreciate how different approaches to conflict influence negotiation.*
- ▶ *Identify ways of becoming a better cross-cultural negotiator.*

The process of bargaining between two or more parties to reach a mutually agreeable solution, according to Dr Yang, can involve the following steps:

1 *Preparation.*
2 *Relationship building.*
3 *Information exchange.*

4 *Persuasion.*
5 *Agreement.*

The final outcome will, however, depend upon the degree of consensus, bargaining ranges, concept of winning, perception of the negotiating process, geographical locations, room arrangement, selection of negotiators, time limits, and so on.

Taking on a world view

How do differences in cultural expectations affect communications? The answer is failure at reading the cues or misreading the cues. So how can you see things from different world views? For instance, at a business lunch if a Brit offers a second helping of a dish to an Arab associate and the latter happens to mutter 'No', the British host will immediately withdraw the plate, because to him/her, a 'No' means a 'No'. But an Arab treating an Arab will go on piling more food on his companion's plate because to him that demonstrates polite hospitality and courteous behaviour.

When there is this kind of clash between cultures, it would be a good idea for members of both cultures to take a more tolerant view of the features of the 'foreign' culture in order for business to be negotiated.

Insight
Take into consideration that a person's world view will have been influenced by their upbringing and culture and that it can be different from your own.

Here are a few tips that Ge Gao and Stella Ting-Toomey (1998) give on overcoming cross-cultural communication roadblocks. Though these tips were drafted for Chinese businessmen, you will see that they can apply as easily to the Arab managers as well in dealing with Europeans:

▶ *Focus on what is being said: try not to read too much into the words or be oversensitive to non-verbal nuances.*
▶ *Learn to accept what is said, is said with their world view.*
▶ *Develop a belief that verbal messages and feedback are powerful and effective.*
▶ *Understand that self-affirmation and individuality are important to North Americans and most Europeans.*
▶ *Be aware that everyone should be treated equally and that polite speech applies to family members, intimate friends and strangers.*
▶ *Accept that many countries (for example, USA, Germany, Sweden, Britain) value direct talk and that requests are often stated explicitly.*
▶ *Recognize that being assertive is only valued in some cultures and that 'No' is not always accepted as an assertive response.*
▶ *Understand that modesty is equated with low self-confidence and that enhancing and crediting oneself is expected in the USA and most European countries but not, for example, in Asia.*
▶ *Learn not to ask personal questions, because they can be offensive and insulting; understand that* guan xing *(to show concern) talk may be considered as meddling and intrusive.*
▶ *Accept that some cultures such as Spanish, French and Italians, like to express their opinions openly and are talkative in their social interactions. Whereas in Asia they are more reserved and less open to expressing their feelings publicly.*

Considering cultural nuances

Culture is the way people live and think. It deeply affects everything they do, including the way of communicating and doing business with each other. A great example of this is the fact that Asians consider harmony an important virtue and will avoid confrontation at all costs. For that reason they will often say 'Yes' to many things with the understanding of 'Yes I hear you' or 'Yes I understand' and not necessarily 'Yes I agree'.

Differences between two cultures in values, perceptions and upbringing can be a source of major misunderstanding. However, with a little tolerance and understanding of the other's perspective it is possible to overcome many of these cultural roadblocks. It is necessary to put aside personal feelings and listen deeply. Developing good listening skills is vital to the understanding of others and their world view. Also, if you are travelling or doing business outside your own culture, doing a little research can go a very long way to preparing a smooth path.

Insight
Be genuinely curious and respectful about others and their way of doing things.

When communicating across cultures put personal feelings and perceptions out of your mind. Listen carefully without judgment and hold your tongue. Avoid comments such as 'Those people' or even worse 'Those foreigners' and stereotypical statements such as 'They can never make decisions' or 'Dealing with them usually means we'll wait forever to get an answer.' Any statements that put a gulf between 'us' and 'them' create disunity and gets you off on the wrong foot.

LANGUAGE INTRICACIES

Be careful about using foreign words unless you are completely sure of their meaning. Similar words in a foreign language can have a completely different meaning. Slightly varying a vowel or the pronunciation of a word can completely alter its intended meaning. Also avoid slang, some phrasal verbs or colloquial expressions.

The following are taken from actual international meetings and speeches:

- *'We've been through the documents with a fine toothcomb.'*
- *'We've come up with zilch, completely hit a brick wall.'*
- *'We couldn't get to the bottom of the problem, it had us totally stumped.'*
- *'Please get this to us ASAP.'*
- *'How can we put this across so that they can grasp it and run with it?'*
- *'Could you give us a ballpark figure?'*
- *'I really feel we are barking up the wrong tree here.'*

You can see by these examples that many people who heard the phrases above will have had no idea of the meaning. Be aware of the background of your audience and their cultural norms. Are they going to be dealing in miles or kilometres? Are you familiar with their currency, beliefs and traditions?

BEHAVIOURAL DIFFERENCES

Study the body language of the country where you are presenting (or of those you are speaking to). Asians do not like to be touched, so grabbing their shoulder and kissing them on both cheeks will be met with dismay. If you are a woman and are kissed by a Spaniard or an Italian on your second meeting, do not be surprised, this is quite normal in their country.

Top tips
- *The only universal gesture is a smile.*
- *There are no rights and wrongs, merely respectful and considerate behaviour.*

Be aware of using gestures that are common in your country but which may be received differently by others. For example, in Western culture you may beckon someone to come over to you from another part of the room. You would hold out your hand and move your fingers towards you gesturing the person to come over. In many countries this would be considered vulgar. Be very sensitive and adapt to the situation you find yourself in as far as possible.

Ensuring clarity

When planning your speech before an international audience it is vitally important to remember to speak clearly and slowly. Pronounce your words by paying special attention to the consonants. By emphasizing them, particularly at the ends of your words, you will greatly improve clarity. The greatest complaint at international conferences is that people speak too fast. Always take into consideration that your audience may not use your language on a daily basis. Even if they do, they may not be used to your own regional accent.

Insight
When you speak, leave out jargon and unfamiliar expressions that may confuse your audience.

Try this as an exercise before you speak to increase the flexibility of your lips and tongue. Taken from *A Christmas Carol* by Charles Dickens:

Oh but he was a tight fisted hand at the grindstone. Scrooge! A squeezing, wrenching, grasping, scraping, clutching, covetous old sinner! Hard and sharp as flint, from which no spark had ever struck out generous fire. Secret and self-contained and solitary as an oyster.

The cold within him froze his old features, nipped his pointed nose, shrivelled his cheek, stiffened his gait; made his eyes red, his lips blue; and spoke out shrewdly in his grating voice...

After you have planned and prepared your speech go through it marking the words and phrases you want to emphasize. Stress the consonants at the ends of your words. Insert the pauses and allow time for your audience to take in what you have said. If you are at a meeting, ask questions to clarify understanding.

Above all, be aware that your preferences and behaviours are culturally based and not necessarily the right ones in a different culture. No international audience will expect you to know all the variations of gestures, body language and communication. All you can do is to keep an open mind to other views and behaviours. This way you will become a successful cross-cultural communicator.

26

···

Presenting to the media

In this chapter you will learn:
- *how to decide on your media plan*
- *how to avoid the pitfalls and 'hot water' situations*
- *how to prepare for the interview.*

Choosing your media strategy

You may need to devise a media plan if:

- ▶ *you are launching a new programme, service or product*
- ▶ *the government has announced a policy you want to protest against*
- ▶ *there's been a new court ruling that affects your company/cause*
- ▶ *you have an interesting report or a study to release*
- ▶ *you have a compelling story to tell*
- ▶ *an important official is visiting your project, company or city*
- ▶ *you want one of your important meetings/seminars/discussions to be covered.*

The media plan that will be most productive for you will depend upon four key questions:

1 *What is your goal?*
2 *Who is your target audience?*

3 *What is your message?*
4 *What resources do you have to execute this plan?*

An effective media strategy requires considerable effort, time and commitment. The size and budget of your organization will also reflect on the success, as well as your choice of an appropriate media vehicle, which would of course depend upon your target audience. For instance, if your organization is involved in spreading the message of effective financial planning to a middle-aged audience, the best mode may be radio broadcasts, but if it's an anti-smoking campaign aimed at young people, you could perhaps try something like the MTV channel. Ideally, if your budget permits, hire a full-time public relations executive to plan events to hang your media releases on. Alternatively, local media students needing work experience may be able to help those on a tighter budget.

Insight
Ask yourself the following question: What is your key message, desired outcome and target audience?

The five Fs of media relations

Insight
When handling the media be: factual, friendly, fair, fast and frank.

1 **Factual:** *Use facts, statistics, dramatic statements, creative slogans, and personal anecdotes.*
2 **Friendly:** *Be courteous and encouraging. Remember journalists' names, read what they write and thank them for their time.*
3 **Fair:** *Treat different news outlets fairly and the same way.*
4 **Fast:** *Respect a journalist's deadlines. When the press calls, assume it is an emergency. A call returned even a few hours later may be too late.*

5 Frank: *Be candid and open. Never mislead journalists. If you can't answer a question, say so. But, try to get back to them with the answers as soon as you can.*

(Source: *A Media Handbook for Creating Social Change*,

Centre for Reproductive Law and Policy)

Be careful – very careful

> **Insight**
> It is usually better to tell the truth and stick to the facts.

Journalists are there to ask challenging questions that will provide a good story. To avoid getting into any kind of 'hot water', take heed of the following:

▶ *Always tell the truth where possible.*

Lying is a cardinal sin. If caught, you will not just lose credibility, it can even turn into a five-inch screaming headline. So, stick to the facts.

▶ *Avoid muttering 'No comment' when trying to wriggle out of a situation.*

This tactic never works. At worst, it will convey the impression that you are hiding something. It might even incite the journalist to pry information out of other sources, who may put a different spin on the issue.

▶ *Say 'I don't know' when you don't know.*

Nobody should expect you to be the *Encyclopaedia Britannica*. Rather than bluff, simply say, 'I'm sorry, I don't know the answer to this one, but I can check and let you know by tomorrow.' Then find out the answer and call back the next day.

▶ *Saying anything 'off the record' can boomerang.*

Whatever you say to a journalist will appear in print, maybe attributed to someone else rather than you. So, unless you are absolutely sure you are ready to share the news with the world, don't divulge.

▶ *Stay cool under all trying circumstances.*

Confrontation with the media is not advisable. The ink that a journalist can throw won't kill, but it can certainly be messy. Pulling a punch at the photographer or news reporter under the glare of media lights may give you a momentary sense of relief, but it will also give you a two-minute unsolicited slot on the national news. Don't risk it!

Communication is rather like riding a seesaw. If a fine balance is not maintained between the listener and the speaker, it will lead to the slow down or collapse of the process.

Insight
Pictures and video clips can be great media hooks, so use them wisely.

MAINTAINING DISTANCE

Dealing with the media is a sensitive issue. Success lies in maintaining an invisible thin line between them and you. It is also crucial that equal amount of importance and respect is given to all media whether it is television, print, radio or the internet. Those who behave differently with different styles of media (perhaps because of the glamour element) always send a poor message across because all branches of the media are closely interlinked and the message spreads.

Also, stick to your promise. If you have promised information at a particular time, abide by that promise. Don't say anything 'off the record' if you are meeting the journalist for the first time. Getting too familiar with a journalist is not advisable; keep matters professional. Eventually familiarity can also breed misunderstandings.

Lastly, it is a great idea to teach telephone techniques to your personal assistant as well. They should know how to take calls from the media. Even if a nosy journalist is pestering and has to be put off, he/she should be turned away firmly but politely. You may need to call them in the future. Refer to Chapter 19 for telephone techniques.

Often a mature journalist will not push you beyond a point but someone who thinks he/she is on the trail of a scoop cannot be sidetracked so easily. In such a situation, the best strategy would be to try a polite but firm means of communicating a negative response. Communicate clearly – this is the key to success. State concisely that you don't have the information at present: *'I'm sorry but I do not have access to this information at present'*, *'I regret that I'm unable to give you any further information'*, *'This is something I am not at liberty to discuss at present.'*

Your press release

A good media release should have the five Ws and an H. It should answer the questions *Who*, *What*, *When*, *Where*, *Why* and *How*. Without these, the message will get lost.

It should also convey your main official agenda:

- ▶ *What do you stand for?*
- ▶ *What are your goals?*
- ▶ *What cause are you championing?*
- ▶ *What message do you ultimately want to convey?*

While writing your press release bare in mind the following points:

- ▶ *Describe your organization accurately and briefly.*
- ▶ *Consider your audience profile.*
- ▶ *Be concise.*
- ▶ *Make sure you leave no big, factual holes or are making any wild sweeping allegations.*

- ▶ *Get a second opinion before you issue your press release so that revisions can be made if required.*
- ▶ *Eliminate all jargon as the idea is to appeal, not to impress.*
- ▶ *Adopt a reasonable, conciliatory tone.*
- ▶ *Make sure your release is typed neatly and is double-spaced. Crumpled or 'tired' releases are sure to land in the nearest bin.*
- ▶ *Include an all-hour contact number and the organization's name and address.*
- ▶ *Ensure that it is carefully edited with no grammatical or spelling mistakes. Consider getting it written or checked by a PR professional.*
- ▶ *Make sure it's free of all jargon.*
- ▶ *Make sure it is simple, clear, accurate and honest.*
- ▶ *Be modest but don't underestimate your accomplishments. If you can't sell yourself, how will you be able to sell your company/cause?*

Top tip

Understand that it's not a journalist's prerogative to decide when, or if at all, your story will get published. That's always the editor's discretion. So, gently remind: 'I am just calling about the press release we sent out to you and wondered if you had received it? Do you think you would be interested in taking it further?'

It is not advisable to pester and if your story still doesn't appear, just give up.

Call a press conference only if you have something new or concrete to say, announce or discuss with the press.

MORE IDEAS FOR MEDIA RELEASES THAT WORK

- ▶ *Provide a 'news peg/hook' – some new angle to a fact or story.*
- ▶ *Use coloured paper so it can be found easily in a heap of other releases.*
- ▶ *Use a headline that gets to the guts of the story, and a first paragraph to summarize content.*

- ▶ *Include quotable quotes from credible sources, along with addresses and email details.*
- ▶ *Include facts, statistics, charts and websites for cross-reference.*
- ▶ *Think pictures. Provide images or sources.*
- ▶ *Work out how to recycle your publicity, especially if someone has written a glowing article about your organization.*
- ▶ *Target the right journalist. Remember, every news report has a pre-assigned place in a newspaper.*
- ▶ *Avoid using 'News Release' or 'For Immediate Release' as a subject line. Grab the journalist's attention with an innovative heading.*
- ▶ *Make sure you avoid incorrect or dated information, especially phone numbers.*
- ▶ *Avoid hyperbolic phrases like 'spectacular', 'incredible', 'one-of-its-kind', 'state-of-the-art', 'cutting-edge' or 'unique breakthrough.' They smack of commercialization.*
- ▶ *Mail or fax your release at least one week in advance of the event. Allow the receiver enough time to schedule and plan for the week's events.*
- ▶ *Avoid pestering the journalist immediately after you have sent the release.*

Giving an interview

So you've got the interview, now what? It is always better to get a few bytes of your presentation recorded and analysed from a media expert before going in for an interview. Think about the kinds of questions you may be asked and prepare them beforehand. Research the background to your company or product as the journalist will expect you to be the expert. If there are any controversial issues be sure of your facts and figures. Note down the key points you would like to get across with contact details.

Insight
In my experience the media always responds well to politeness and a winning smile.

ACHIEVING GOOD BYTES

Here are some top tips:

▸ *One of the following elements should ideally be there in the byte: revealing facts/statements, authoritative comments, feelings of people connected to the story. Remember that all bytes must carry the interview forward.*

▸ *Give only the authentic information. Don't hypothesize or do any guesswork.*

▸ *Ensure you know where to look when the camera is on.*

▸ *Switch off your mobile phone.*

▸ *Holding a mike is a reporter's privilege. Avoid snatching it from his/her hand when you start speaking.*

▸ *Do not interrupt the person until he is finished with whatever he has to say, even if you are dying to wedge in a sound byte of your own.*

▸ *Appear attentive while recording the byte. Nod or gesticulate, expressing amazement or whatever you feel. Try to be a perfect listener for the camera.*

▸ *If you think you have a very good point to make, don't hesitate to reiterate. Slow down, take a deep breath and reiterate, just once.*

▸ *Feel comfortable with the camera, and while the shoot is on look directly at the interviewer.*

In an audio-visual medium, looks and speech are both important, so try to strike a balance between the two. Do some facial exercises on a regular basis and practise tongue twisters. 'Red leather yellow leather' said fast is a good one, as is 'Six thick thistle sticks' and 'Round rugged rock ragged rascals ran'. Try saying these ten times.

Top tip
> Wear a smile for every season, even without a reason. Sometimes even flawless diction and a great personality are not good substitutes for a smiling disposition.

APPEARANCE

Not all television channels have a make-up artist available for guests, so put some light make-up on yourself before heading for the studio. Ask the interviewer/producer in advance which colour to wear or which colour might clash with his/her sets. Ask even if this question makes you feel embarrassed. Think of what effect a canary yellow dress can have against a maroon background!

Unless you have specifically been asked to, do not wear anything that is multi-layered. Note that pure white, black, and thin stripes do not work well on set, but wear darker colours if you are at all self-conscious about your figure. Also remember, you can hide a multitude of sins behind the table.

UNDERSTANDING THE DRILL

Study the studio jargon. For instance, you must know what a lapel (a small microphone) is and how to wear one when the studio hand asks you to.

Ask the producer where you should look while talking. Normally there are more than two cameras in the studio and you must know your 'looking room' when the recording is on. Concentrate on your body language and facial expressions. At no point should your attitude appear negative or lethargic. Speak with full authority and confidence (pause and remember to breathe! – see Chapters 1, 2 and 3).

If there are other guests on the panel, listen to them closely when they speak. Watch your reactions and expressions. The camera might just capture those shots.

Ask the cameraman to point out the position in which you must be sitting, so that he/she doesn't end up taking all your shots in profile.

During the interview answer the questions concisely and then remain silent. Here are further tips to bear in mind. Remember to do the breathing exercises in Chapter 2.

- *Refer to concrete examples, personal anecdotes and clear images to illustrate your point.*
- *Remember, journalists want stories as well as data.*
- *Never assume that a journalist agrees with you.*
- *Eliminate acronyms from your speech.*
- *Be persuasive, honest, energetic and enthusiastic.*
- *Do not worry about the silent pauses. Sometimes they are an effective tool to allow the message to sink in, and can look quite dramatic on TV with the right person, at the right time, for the right purpose.*
- *Tell the journalist what you think is the most important point you have made.*
- *Try to relax and enjoy the moment. Harness any nervousness and use it to add emotion and a sense of conviction to your voice.*
- *Above all, be honest and genuine because the camera has sharp eyes – it can catch your inner thoughts.*
- *Remember to thank the interviewer (and crew if appropriate).*

27

Sales presentations

In this chapter you will learn:
- *how to sell experiences*
- *how to discover what the customer wants*
- *how to ask questions rather than provide answers*
- *how to close the sale.*

If you were listening to a sales pitch which of these would you prefer?

> *Here's a great chair, it has a leather seat for comfort and is easy to adjust to suit any height. It gives good back and neck support and the price is very competitive.*

Or

> *I sold two of these chairs last week to a family in Leeds. The husband, who had a minor back problem, bought one for himself and one for his mother. They liked the competitive price but what they liked most was the great soft leather seat and the flexible height adjustment which really supported their backs.*

Generally, people enjoy hearing about personal experiences and would choose the second pitch. You can identify with the story and imagine the people sitting in the chair and feeling the support and comfort. Look at the second example in a car showroom:

I have a great <u>little</u> car here that would suit you. It is the latest <u>dark</u> green, <u>automatic</u>, has powered steering, a great CD player, electric windows...bla bla (and so on). The price is only £7,995 on the road.

Or

Good morning, what kind of car are you looking for? Oh I see you <u>don't like automatics</u> and would only consider <u>very pale</u> colours. Oh and you have children so you would like <u>an estate</u> (the assistant listened to the customer). Well my sister finds this one suits her perfectly as she has three children... (and so on)

Insight

Think about selling stories rather than products and services.

Your sales pitch

Top tip

People do not buy products they buy experiences.

However, keep a balance as most people don't like waffle either and do not take kindly to long stories.

If you can, allow people to talk before trying the sales pitch. You will find out a lot about their needs and requirements. This way you will save a great deal of time and energy. It is no use applying great sales patter, only to discover that they don't want that particular product or feature. When people talk about themselves it will help them to relax. They will see that you are interested in them and want the best for them rather than trying to 'close' a sale as quickly as possible.

Find where their needs are and then give them the solution. Tell them why this solution will be beneficial for them.

This is an example when selling a service:

You have been speaking to a potential customer and have asked several questions. They are obviously quite busy and you noticed that they had arrived late.

Potential customer: So what do you do exactly?

You: **Well, you know when** people are really busy and find it difficult to keep on top of things (the problem), **what I do is** present one-off time management seminars (solution) **so that** people can go away with useful strategies that really work. This saves them valuable time and energy (benefits).

Follow this up with questions to find out more, or they may now be interested enough to ask you!

Avoid telling people what you do first. Instead begin with 'Well, you know when…' to catch their imagination. Then solve the problem with what you do, 'What I do is…' Then sell the benefits 'so that…'.

There is no point in guessing what the customer wants, it has to be what they need. Ask the 'Ws and H' questions to find out more about their needs. For example:

- ▶ *'What kind of … do you want?'*
- ▶ *'Where will you be using/needing it?'*
- ▶ *'Who will be using/needing it?'*
- ▶ *'Why do you need/want it?'*
- ▶ *'When do you need it by?'*
- ▶ *'How much do you want to spend?'*

Selling the benefits

Note: It is advisable to read Chapters 1, 2 and 3 before proceeding.

You are not really selling a product or service you are selling the benefits. What does it represent and what can it do for your customers? When people buy a watch it's not the watch they want it's the ability to tell the time and the features. Connect to people's feelings. Explain to an older audience the useful expanding strap with no fiddly fixations. The fact that the watch is powered by light and needs no battery may also be useful for them. To a younger audience point out the trendy watch-face and different colour options they can choose from. Spend time building rapport and making the audience feel at ease. Then you really will see an increase in sales.

UNDERSTANDING YOUR CUSTOMER

When people trust you and feel they know you they will also want to buy from you. How many people drive miles for their own trusted builder, doctor or hairdresser? If they have had good service in the past and trust the service they will always return.

The more you understand your customer and their needs the easier it is to convince them that your product is the right one for them. Consider how your product or service could be adapted to suit your customer's needs. Show your audience how it would be of benefit to them if they changed to your product or service.

If you are using slides make them highly visual. Even if you are selling a 'dry' service or technical products your slides need to 'show' as your words are telling.

Insight
If you can show, tell, demonstrate and allow people to experience your product or service, you will have a head start.

IMAGES AND THE REAL THING

If you are selling mobile phones, for example, have coloured slides of the main features. Allow people to see what your product can deliver and the benefits. Slide after slide with bullet points and clever headlines are no substitute for being able to visualize the benefits.

If possible, demonstrate your products in front of your audience. If space allows invite your audience to come up and handle the products. If you are able to give away some samples this is a sure way for the audience to remember you.

You may think you are unable to demonstrate a service but, with a little imagination, this can also be possible. If you are promoting a secretarial or PA service you may demonstrate by bringing in an untidy and overloaded 'in-tray' and then showing a reduced and tidy one beside it. You could use juggling balls to show how people try to 'juggle' too many tasks. There are always imaginative ways to demonstrate both products and services.

ENTHUSIASM FOR THE PRODUCT

Carry your enthusiasm into the presentation and use creative vocabulary. It is motivating for your audience to hear colourful adjectives when you describe your product or service. Keep your energy going until you speak your last word and leave them with a startling fact or benefit:

▶ *'This is one of the best products on the market for pain relief. It has had a wonderful reception and now you have a chance to experience the amazing benefits.'*
▶ *'This is one of our most popular customer care courses and the benefits to the participants are shown in the highly complimentary feedback forms we have received.'*
▶ *'The impact of this product on the market is truly remarkable. No other product has beaten us on quality and price. The benefits are amazing and sales are booming.'*

Closing the sale

If you are doing a sales presentation the 'sale' is best left until you are able to speak on a one-to-one basis. Set up a personal conversation with the audience members. Make sure you have your promotional materials available and can show people on the day. This will avoid having to send them on later.

Selling is the transfer of your own enthusiasm for your product or service. Passion and genuine enthusiasm sells. If you love what you sell you are almost there, as people buy products and services from people who promote with energy. If you have created a situation where the customer is interested, just assume that the sale will go ahead. If you have asked your questions and found out their needs you will have shown how your product or service can benefit them. Here are some suggestions when closing the sale.

To allow the customer to let you know if there are any outstanding issues, ask:

▶ *'Well it seems as if we could proceed. Do you have any more questions?'*
▶ *'Well I am happy to proceed, what do you think?'*

If they want the product but the cost is the issue, ask:

▶ *'We are facing rising costs and this is the final batch/service we can sell at this price. If you can make a decision today we can let you have it for the lower rate. What do you think?'*

Offer an incentive to draw people away from your competitors:

▶ *'In order to demonstrate our commitment we can offer you a free service contact (or equivalent) for the first year, would that be of interest?'*
▶ *'If you would be interested in speaking to XY company, who is a good customer, we could set up a meeting. Would this be something you would like to go ahead with?'*

Finally, when the sale is almost on the table, assume it is all going ahead and ask confidently:

▶ *'So when would you like us to deliver?'*
▶ *'Which one did you decide on/option did you go for?'*
▶ *'So when can we set this up for you?'*
▶ *'When would you like to finalize the details/contract?'*

Either/or questions also work well:

▶ *'Do you want the first or the second option?'*
▶ *'Would you like that in the leather or the wood?'*

When asking for payment be confident and to the point:

▶ *'Will payment be by cheque or credit card?'*
▶ *'Would you like to pay by bank transfer or by cheque?'*
▶ *'What is your preferred method of payment?'*

Insight

If you believe in the product or service, so will your customers.

LOSING THE SALE

What happens if you didn't manage to close the sale?

Do an evaluation and ask yourself:

- ▶ *Why didn't I close the sale?*
- ▶ *Did I clearly identify the need?*
- ▶ *Was I speaking to the wrong person?*
- ▶ *Have I covered all the benefits and features?*

If you know where things went wrong you can easily put this right. Be totally honest with yourself, as everyone learns by making mistakes. Search for ways of improving your techniques. Were you confident and enthusiastic? How could you improve your presentation next time round?

FOLLOWING UP THE SALE

It always pays to follow up a sale. Customers are usually pleased when you keep in touch and this is the time to get valuable feedback. Again, ask questions to find out how the product or service is benefiting them. (Always assuming it is!)

Send them updates on your products or service so you are in their minds when making repeat orders. Long-term relationships are worth nurturing and can guarantee sales for years to come.

To conclude with a quote is a useful strategy for all speeches so here is an example taken from an article by Sam Silverman:

> *If you're going into a speech you need to set standards for yourself so you can determine later whether you reached your targets. In business, set standards for your performance, so you will rise with insight and purpose to each new level of accomplishment.*

10 THINGS TO REMEMBER

1 *At business events, decide what information the attendees need to hear. Decide on your objectives and the outcomes you want.*

2 *Delegate some of the preparation to your colleagues. If you do this, delegate with clear deadlines.*

3 *Allow opinions to be voiced. Listen respectfully to comments and questions.*

4 *Keep to the agenda and the schedule.*

5 *Prepare all documentation well in advance.*

6 *Follow up on any action points agreed.*

7 *When speaking for an international audience, consider any cultural differences both with regard the content of your speech and the format the speech takes.*

8 *Avoid slang, idioms and phrasal verbs. Non-verbal signals can be very revealing or misunderstood. The only universal gesture is a smile.*

9 *During a sales presentation, expand on facts but keep waffle to a minimum. Enlarge on the benefits to the customer.*

10 *Close the sale with confidence and enthusiasm, and remember, it always pays to follow up a sale.*

Part six

And finally...

28

Avoiding pitfalls

In this chapter you will learn:
- *how to avoid drying up*
- *how to combat nerves and nausea*
- *how to recover if you 'bomb'*
- *how to cope if the technology fails.*

Just before you step onto a stage to speak you tend to focus on yourself: 'How will people perceive me?', 'Will I be a success?', 'Have I prepared enough?' and so on. There are other mutterings in the back of your mind: 'Am I good enough?', 'Do they really want to listen to me?', 'I am not nearly as good as the last speaker'. These thoughts all contribute to the possibility of 'drying up' as they are eating away at your confidence.

Insight
It is true that a positive, confident voice sends a positive, confident message.

Thinking positively

Now, let's look at the kind of alternative messages you could be giving yourself. Firstly, consider those positive affirmations you read about in the first three chapters. Then focus on your audience – taking the pressure off yourself. If you really want them to have the information or entertainment they came for then focus on your message. Channel those nerves into energy and excitement. Look out at the audience and breathe in, allowing yourself to stay calm and focused. Then you will not have time to worry about yourself.

Before you speak make sure you place a glass of water nearby (somewhere you can easily get to). If you start to forget your words, walk over and take a sip of water. All good speakers deal with these moments calmly. It doesn't mean they never stumble. It's OK to be nervous and it's fine if you pause to remember your words. The secret is to make your audience think you paused on purpose. Building in pauses and times to sip water is a sure way of helping you to stay fluent. Stand with the silence, allow it to be there with you for a moment, trust that you will be able to continue and you will. As soon as you start trusting your own ability things will improve and grow.

If you feel nervous this is perfectly normal. Use your nerves and channel them to say these affirmations to yourself:

▶ *'I am nervous and this enables me to be enthusiastic and energized.'*
▶ *'Many great actors are physically sick before a performance, I am in good company.'*
▶ *'I am able to get over these nerves and replace them with passion.'*
▶ *'I am bound to succeed as I have planned, prepared and practised.'*

Create your own affirmations using positive statements in the present tense as those above.

Improving all the time

Insight
Your speaking ability will improve the more you speak – it is just like a muscle, it needs exercise!

If you 'bomb' after a speech you hoped would move or inspire your audience ask yourself:

▶ *What could I have done better?*
▶ *What exactly was it that went wrong?*
▶ *How can I avoid that in future?*
▶ *Was it all me or was this audience particularly difficult?*
▶ *What actions will I now take to ensure this is not repeated?*

It does not help to dwell too long on a speech that did not go according to plan. There are times when some speeches go well for one audience and not for another. That's just how it is. If you think things through and answer the questions above you will only improve next time. Think about this as an opportunity to learn about your style and material. Get some feedback from a colleague if you can. It is useful to hear from others how you come across and then move forward with this valuable information. You will constantly improve as public speaking is like anything else, it needs practice and patience to perfect.

Insight

Remember that one successful speech does not always have the same impact on a different audience – variety is key.

Common problems

The most common disaster when giving a PowerPoint presentation or using slides is when the technology fails. You have done everything to ensure the different pieces of equipment are in full working order. You have checked them and all is working well. Then during the presentation it all breaks down – you feel frustrated and all your hard work is jeopardized. Or is it? Let's check and see:

Beforehand you asked yourself, 'What do I do if the technology fails?'

You then:

- *backed up your slides or PowerPoints with printed handouts*
- *knew the material well and could talk it through*
- *printed some key sections out in larger format*
- *carried with you a memory stick, some pens, scissors, Sellotape and extension leads*
- *decided that if the equipment broke down you would stay calm and carry on.*

Zig Ziglar, one of the highest paid sales speakers in America, said:

> **It's not your aptitude but your attitude that will determine your altitude.**

If you have the attitude that nothing can stand in the way of your speech or presentation then you will pull through. If you always ask yourself 'What if…', you will be prepared for every eventuality.

- *What if I forget a piece of vital equipment?*
- *What if I leave my notes behind?*
- *What if the venue is not prepared?*
- *What if only half the audience turn up?*
- *What if I forget my speech?*

All these 'what if's' have been addressed in the previous chapters. If you plan and prepare for every 'what if' you can think of, then you will always have a back-up plan. This realization will free you up to face any crisis or lapse of memory. You will feel confident in the knowledge that you have covered all possibilities.

Insight

It is really advisable to check all equipment several times and be prepared for it to fail – it often does.

Final word

If you have been asked to make a speech or a presentation, start
planning it now. If you have the desire to deliver a seminar, take
that first step. Speaking in public is serious fun. People begin
to value your ideas and your opinions matter. This will have a
direct impact on your organization and your own professional
reputation.

As a keen skier I am able to relate my speaking experiences to
standing at the top of a mountain looking down. Have you ever
skied? Do you know that feeling? Perhaps you have been a
climber facing the first rock, or a swimmer who was afraid of
the water? How did you manage to face that fear? How many
times did you fall back and start over again? Speaking in front
of any audience takes practice too. You will have great moments
and daunting ones. You will face down that mountain as a
speaker and your knees will feel weak. Once you have done it a
few times you will gain confidence and cast aside those doubts.
You will fall flat on your face in the snow, you will sink in the
water, and you will graze your knees on the rock face. But, you'll
try again and then next time it's a little easier. It's all part of
the challenge.

In *Tao of Personal Leadership* Diane Dreher writes:

> *We've gone through life developing quite a good record of doing things we've never done before: learning to walk, to talk, to read and write. To drive a car and many other skills we probably now take for granted. At one time each of them was a new challenge.*

The Tao tells us that a journey of a thousand miles begins with a single step. The path of human progress has been cleared one step at a time, by those who dared to reach out to new possibilities, to do what they'd never done before.

In summary, here's a great quote from D. Walters that is brief and clear:

> *Success is not a doorway, it's a stairway.*

10 THINGS TO REMEMBER

1 *Use positive affirmations, as they build confidence.*

2 *Visualize yourself being successful.*

3 *If you dry up, pause, breathe, take a drink and resume.*

4 *Learn from your mistakes. Ask what you could do better next time.*

5 *Some speeches will go well, others not so well. That's how it is.*

6 *Move on and take the learning points forward.*

7 *Ensure that everything is prepared and checked over in advance.*

8 *Make a list of 'What ifs' and then act accordingly.*

9 *Your speaking journey, like any other, needs you to take the first step.*

10 *'Success is not a doorway, it's a stairway.' D. Walters.*

Taking it further

So you have placed your toe firmly in the water of public speaking, but can you swim out there in the sea? Reading about making a great speech can help you to tame your trepidation. It can provide you with useful tips and techniques to try out. Now it is time to launch yourself off that springboard into the fascinating depths, and to use the PPPs to impress even the most sceptical of fish!

The good news is that there are public speaking clubs all over the world where novice speakers can hone their skills. Many quite expert speakers also join up to perfect their techniques and gain practice in front of a ready-made audience. Most speakers' clubs offer a fantastic training programme and there are mentors to support new members.

Toastmasters International has clubs in most major cities and the joining fee is very reasonable indeed. **The Association of Speakers Clubs** also welcomes new members, and details of the websites for both are below. There is no pressure to speak to begin with. You can ask questions, offer a suggestion or just go and observe. After a couple of meetings, set yourself a target of one speech at the end of the month, after all you will only gain confidence by plunging in and testing the water. You do not need to be an aspiring public speaker. Many people join for a specific occasion or to feel more confident in groups or at meetings.

If you want to speak professionally it is a good idea to contact local charities (that are always happy to have good speakers). The Rotary Clubs, Lions Clubs and the WI are all examples. Amnesty International and Save the Children are also charities that often look for speakers. Offer your service free until you feel confident enough to start charging.

I live by the sea and love diving under the waves, even when the water is freezing cold. After a little while the body gets used to the water and the exhilaration you feel when swimming and floating is wonderful. Speaking is very similar. At first the prospect of diving in seems daunting but as soon as you warm up and relax you will begin to enjoy it. People will listen attentively and you will feel the buzz of a speech well delivered. So enjoy the experience, be your authentic self and get out there and let that self be heard.

Further reading

Jackie Arnold, *Raise Your Glasses Please*, How To Books (2007)
Philippa Davies, *Total Confidence*, Piatkus Books (1995)
Lee Glickstein, *Be Heard Now*, Broadway Books (2001)
Bill McFarlan, *Drop the Pink Elephant*, Capstone (2003)
Christina Stuart, *Speak For Yourself*, Piatkus Books (2001)
Lilyan Wilder, *7 Steps to Fearless Speaking*, John Wiley & Sons (1999)

For business presentations
Eric Maisel, *Fearless Presenting*, Backstage Books (1997)
Doug Stevenson, *Never Be Boring Again*, Cornelia Press (2003)

Useful websites

www.toastmasters.org
Toastmasters International is a non-profit organization offering proven – and enjoyable – ways to practise communication skills.

www.the-asc.org.uk
The Association of Speakers Clubs.

www.nsaspeaker.org
The National Speakers Association for Professional Speakers.

The author's details

Website
www.coach4executives.com
A site containing speaking and presenting tips and e-books as well as courses in development coaching and mentoring.

Previous publications
Jackie Arnold, *Raise Your Glasses Please*, How To Books (2007)

Jackie Arnold, *Coaching for Leaders in the Workplace*, How To Books (2009)

Course writer for Coaching and Mentoring Qualifications at Levels 3 and 5 (2004–2008), Institute of Leadership and Management (ILM)

Examinations writer for London Chamber of Commerce and Industry Examinations Board (LCCIEB) (1989–2000), English for Business and Tourism

Contributor of Business English Workshops for 'Languages for Specific Purposes', CILT Kingston University (1994)

Index

Image credits

Notes

Notes

Notes

Notes

Notes

Notes